COUCHSURFING: THE MUSICAL

COUCHSURFING:

The Musical

A travel memoir
by

GARY PEDLER

Adelaide Books
New York / Lisbon
2019

COUCHSURFING: THE MUSICAL
A travel memoir
By Gary Pedler

Copyright © by Gary Pedler
Cover design © 2019 Adelaide Books

Published by Adelaide Books, New York / Lisbon
adelaidebooks.org
Editor-in-Chief
Stevan V. Nikolic

For any information, please address Adelaide Books
at info@adelaidebooks.org
or write to:
Adelaide Books
244 Fifth Ave. Suite D27
New York, NY, 10001

ISBN-10: 1-950437-39-6
ISBN-13: 978-1-950437-39-9

Printed in the United States of America

To Stewart, who told me to write it

Contents

Foreword

I don't intend this book as an endorsement of Couchsurfing.com, which has changed a great deal since I made the trip described in this book, or any other particular organization. What interests me is the idea of someone welcoming a stranger into his home as a guest, regardless of the particular channel used for arranging this.

Prologue – Do I Hear a Musical?

I stood at the entrance to an apartment block in Tel Aviv, hunting for a name on a big panel of intercom buttons. The name probably wasn't all that difficult to spot, but it had been a long day, and I was both tired and on edge. What should have been a straightforward trip here from Amman had gone awry. The bus had stopped at the border. The line inside the Israeli customs building was clogged by a mass of elderly Indian tourists, and by the time I finally managed to exit from the other side, the bus had taken off without me. A young German woman who was also stranded and spoke some Arabic called the bus company and browbeat it into sending us a taxi that got us at least as far as Nazareth. From there, guided by a map I'd hand-drawn from a Google map on my computer and that looked like the work of a seven-year-old, I managed to make my way to this northern suburb of Tel Aviv.

I was about to Couchsurf for the first time.

A couple of years before, I'd created a profile on Couchsurfing.com, then done absolutely nothing with it. Finally, during this around the world trip that had started in Asia two months before, I'd contacted local Couchsurfers and met them for coffee or a drink, in Singapore, Mumbai, Amman. That was getting my toe wet. At present, I was paddling my surfboard out into the water and about to get thoroughly soaked. Assuming I could just find my host's goddamned name somewhere on this goddamned panel. . . .

For those of you who don't already know, here's how Couchsurfing works. I'm planning to visit Destination X. I send some potential hosts in the area Couch Requests asking if I can stay with them on such-and-such dates. If a host accepts my request, we work out the details of when I'll arrive and by what means: bus, train, bicycle, pogo stick. "It's like Airbnb," people say when I explain the system. Kind of, except for the important point that there's no exchange of money. Imagine that, in our hyper-commercialized world, a situation in which you're specifically instructed not to pay for something.

When I first heard about Couchsurfing, if someone had told me that I would become a surfer with almost fifty stays under my belt, let alone write a book on the subject, I would have laughed long and hard. Spend the night in the home of some stranger, probably not even in my own room? No thanks, not my cup of tea. As a teenager, I'd rejoiced when my parents let my brother move into our guest room, leaving me in sole possession of the bedroom we'd shared. Applying for a college dorm room, I'm sure I made a heavy check mark next to "single room." Moving to San Francisco, I lived alone in a studio apartment for twelve years, where the *tang tang* of the cable cars on Powell Street compensated for sleeping on a rickety old Murphy bed. As an adult, I didn't finally live with someone until my partner persuaded me to cohabit, and then only with the inducement that I got to live in a charming bay-windowed Victorian. However, desperation is the mother of invention, and standing there in front of the intercom panel, with its rows of names handwritten in faded ink, I was semi-desperate.

I should explain how I came to be circumnavigating the globe. My mother had died five years after my father, leaving me enough money to take an extended break from the work world. My ex had made his farewells a short while before, after fifteen years of civil partnership – mainly civil, though we did have our lapses. Without much to keep me in San Francisco, I headed west.

I had some money, but not a lot, and needed to travel on a short, thin shoestring. Once I put Asia behind me, I moved into a less budget-friendly part of the world, starting with Israel, with Europe looming beyond. Some people would say the obvious solution was to stay in hostels. However, I agreed with Sartre, who declared after spending several tortured nights at *Les Deux Magots Hostel*: "Hell is other people . . . in a hostel." The people who returned to a dorm room at midnight without having put out a single thing they needed to get ready for bed. The Bag Rustlers who had stashed all their belongings in plastic bags and, in the first light of dawn, fiddled with them for what seemed like hours. Hunched over my laptop in my hotel room in Amman and planning the next leg of my trip, I felt I had to take at least a tentative sip of what I didn't believe was my cup of tea. After reading every word in each profile for hosts in Tel Aviv, studying any photographs included either of the person or the lodging, I sent out my first requests.

You may ask what in the world someone in his fifties thinks he's doing, writing a book about Couchsurfing. Other writing on the subject tends to feature very young people reeling among the homes of other very young people. "Grabbed a beer" is the most frequently recurring phrase, followed by "grabbed another beer." For those in their early twenties, Couchsurfing is a natural extension of crashing at a friend-of-a-friend's place because you don't have enough money or planning ability to do anything else. I'm here to make a case that Couchsurfing can work equally well for us older folk. I do it, you can do it, even families with kids do it.

You may also ask what inspired the title of this book. To answer, I have to shift ahead to a later travel destination, Vienna. In one of its many attempts to squeeze publicity juice out of its most famous painter, the city was plastered with posters advertising *Gustav Klimt: das Musical.* I never saw this show, and conceivably it was a work of genius, the *Monday in the Wienerwald with Gustav* of musical theater. However, the bare idea sounded absurd. According to a synopsis, the climax of the first act ran as follows:

> Gustav, now driven by his Genius [Genius apparently being a character in the show], withdraws from the Künstlerhaus-Collective, which is dominated by conservative powers, and creates the Vienna Secession. The construction of a modern exhibition building as a home for the new art movement is decided upon. Above the entrance is written: "To every age its art and to art its freedom."

Can't you just picture it? A one-third scale model of the Secession Building descends from the fly space and the chorus tap dances its way down the front steps crowing, "To every age its art, And to art its freeee-dom!" Curtain, thunderous applause!

Exploring Vienna, I amused myself by making up crazy titles that ended in "the Musical." *Kaffee mit Schlag: the Musical. Gum on the Sidewalk: the Musical.* This proved dangerous, for when I got the idea of writing this book and asked myself what to call it, the title came to me at once and I couldn't dislodge it.

As for how I intend to relate Couchsurfing and musicals, all I'll say for the moment is that I've always been a fan of musicals and would love to write one. I did once start the book and lyrics for a musical called *Sunday Cowboys*. This was based on nights spent in a gay Country-Western dance club that was only open on Sundays. After twenty pages, it dawned on me that, of all my works that were unlikely ever to come before the public, a musical would top the list. Partly because I didn't have a composer to write the score, who in any case to achieve my musical ideals would need to be a mix of Franz Lehár, Leonard Bernstein, and Johnny Cash.

I'll quote what seems to me the best, or at any rate the least awful, passage from *Sunday Cowboys*. Max, originally from New Orleans, is giving a dance class, assisted by Pistol, a nickname I took from an old Western. Dancing together leads to a flashback of their first roll in the hay, with Max the classic More Interested Party, Pistol the Less So.

> While the other dancers continue the Shadow Dance in the background, Max and Pistol separate and stand still. The lighting on them changes to emphasize that what follows takes place in their past.

MAX (giddy)
That was fantastic!

PISTOL (matter of fact)
Yeah, I enjoyed it.

> Their dialogue edges into song.

MAX
Like getting shot to the moon,
In a polka dot balloon.

PISTOL
I really enjoyed it.

MAX
Like fireworks and shooting stars,
Bumper cars and soft guitars.

PISTOL
It was swell, my little mint julep.

MAX
Like potato chips and caviar,
Like Frenchmen with *beaucoup de savoir*.

PISTOL
We gave each other quite a working over.

MAX
Like a fast ride in a funicular,
Like so many things, it's quite bizarre.

PISTOL
We left no stone unturned.

MAX
It was something ocular, glandular
Singular, spectacular,
And something to keep,

Yes, definitely to keep
In my standard repertoire!

Max later sings a peppy song about surviving Hurricane Katrina. . . . But enough for now.

At last I found the name I was looking for on the panel, that of my first Couchsurfing host, Amnon. My index finger traversed the space between me and one of the buttons. With a tingle of fear-excitement in my chest, I said half out loud, "Okay, here we go."

Chapter 1

Israel: Fiddler on the Roof

AMNON

Up on the seventh floor, Amnon shook my hand and waved me into his apartment. I carried my wheeled suitcase inside rather than pulling it, not wanting to run the slightest risk of damaging his floor: not a good way to start a visit. Amnon was fifty-eight, according to his profile. I add this proviso since in my own profile, I shaved five years off my age. I already felt out of place among the youngsters who dominated Couchsurfing, though to reduce from fifty-five to fifty might not help much. Amnon was short, with short arms and short fingers. He had a round face covered with a graying beard and a rotund body.

Like someone losing his virginity, I'd chosen my first host with special care to ensure a good initiatory experience. The appeal of Amnon was that he was close to my age, a professor, and – let me admit – that he offered a private room. As I gained more experience as a Couchsurfer, I found this was an advantage to staying with older hosts, that they tended to offer better accommodations. To generalize: with hosts in their twenties, you got the floor next to their bed where you could unroll a sleeping bag; with those in their thirties, you rose higher on the comfort scale and got a couch in the living room; with those in their forties and above, you might attain the Couchsurfing heaven of your own bedroom.

Amnon had a late class to teach at Tel Aviv University and seemed pleased by my suggestion that I accompany him; either because this was more convenient or because he had qualms about leaving a stranger alone in his apartment and giving him a key, as I would have in his position. Or at least as I would have before I became used to the ways of Couch-surfing.

On the road, Amnon exclaimed at other drivers' stupidity, making impatient gestures. "Israeli drivers are notoriously bad," he said. "And so am I," he added with a smile. Before heading off to his class, Amnon showed me where his office was in case I wanted to go online using his computer.

Instead, I mooched around the campus. At times while searching for hosts, I'd asked myself if I was cut out for Couch-surfing. At my worst, I was shy, finicky, and inflexible, all qualities that worked against being a good surfer. Later, I realized that in some ways, I might actually not be such a bad candidate. I was perfectly willing to do things that weren't typically touristic, like exploring a university campus.

In one building, I ate some crackers sitting among the students gathered in the lobby. Most of the young women, with dark hair and pale skin, resembled Jewish women I'd known in the U.S. Growing up in Napa Valley, I was used to Jewish people being a spice added to a mainly Protestant-Catholic dish. Israel presented me with a country in which *I* was the spice, the small minority.

I thought of my high school staging *Fiddler on the Roof* in my junior year. I imagined that when the show's creators were trying to drum up interest in their project in the early Sixties, more than one potential backer exclaimed, "You want to make a musical about Jewish peasants in pre-revolutionary Russia, ending with them getting deported? You must be crazy!" Even when it was a success on Broadway, who would have supposed it would become such a popular musical among community groups and high schools over the years? No doubt it helped that Tevye had three daughters to marry off rather than three sons, since in those settings talented women were in greater supply.

Originally assigned to the chorus like most juniors, I'd had my lucky break when the senior who'd snagged the role of Mendel, the rabbi's son, walked out of rehearsals in a huff, bristling at the demands of the choir director, Mr. Richards. My big moment came when I rushed on stage during a village dance and shouted, "The Russians are coming!" or words to that effect. After hearing me in this scene for the first time, Mr. Richards, perhaps fearing another walk out, tried to be gentle. "Now Gary, you have this nice small quiet voice, but you've got to fill this whole theater with it."

For our production, all that blondish brown hair that predominated in my home town had to be dyed black, and black beards and mustaches glued on the males. Having always been partial to men with dark hair, I was delighted to be transformed into one myself for the three performances. The black hair made me attractive, the beard turned me into an adult, a prayer shawl transformed me into a turn-of-the-century Jew living in the shtetl of Anatevka. . . .

I noticed I wasn't the only non-Jew hanging out in the lobby. Two Muslim girls talked together, recognizable by their headscarves. In answer to my naive-outsider question, Amnon had said that of course Israeli Arabs attended the university, though they often had problems with their Hebrew, since their earlier schooling was in Arabic.

When we returned to his apartment, Amnon offered me wine and whiskey. I said no thanks to both. Amnon drank whiskey himself. "Just a small amount," he said, holding up his glass. "It isn't good for my health to drink a lot."

Amnon told me a little about his background. He was born in Poland. For political reasons, the Polish leader Władysław Gomułka had allowed Jewish emigration from there in the late Fifties. Amnon's parents came to Israel, leaving most of their possessions behind. His father, who had been a civil servant, started by hauling sacks at Jaffa Port. His mother, a nurse-practitioner, had to work as an orderly.

"My family wasn't religious," Amnon said. "I didn't even know I was Jewish when we arrived. The main reason to come was that my mother's only remaining sibling lived here, a sister. The others had died in the Holocaust. Family was important to my mother."

As a child, Amnon cut school all the time and went to the library, where he had a desk "reserved" for him by the librarians. "I read anything I came across, compulsively," he said, "even a veterinary manual. The librarians never asked why I wasn't at school and never told me I was reading something I shouldn't."

I was surprised to find that Amnon, a professor, hadn't done well in school. "At least not in subjects that involved rote learning, like languages," he said. "My brain just doesn't work that way. I didn't become a good student until I was at university, studying the right subjects. I got a triple major in Anthropology, Psychology, and Sociology."

Amnon attended graduate school in Boston and married a fellow Israeli. "We could have stayed in the States, but we didn't want to raise our daughter there. For one thing, we didn't like the obsession with school sports, the cheerleaders and all that." Back in Israel, he and his wife eventually divorced. His daughter was currently studying in the same three fields he had. "She's an improved version of me," Amnon said with a sweet smile.

Amnon collaborated with Polish colleagues in his research work. "My closest friends are Poles, not Israelis. I speak Polish at the level of an eight-year-old. When I talk with Poles about anything difficult, we switch to English."

I asked Amnon if he'd considered immigrating to Poland. "I immigrated once in my life," he said. "That was enough. Though I'm glad my daughter can have Polish citizenship if she wants." This was to become a recurring motif in my talks with Israelis, that while they or their parents might have come to Israel, they often had more or less concrete plans to move again, sometimes back to the same places their forebearers had fled.

Amnon and I grazed on bags of snack foods he'd spread over the kitchen table. "I can't put anything away," he said. "It's part of my ADD." He left open most of the cupboard doors in the kitchen. Maybe that was another part.

After he consumed a small amount of whiskey, Amnon poured himself other small amounts. I worried he might get tipsy, but he didn't seem strongly affected, except in a certain excitability. We had a long talk about Israeli history and politics. Far into the conversation, I asked Amnon:

"If you could go back in time and had the power, would you prevent the creation of Israel?"

"No," he said. "Israel was absolutely necessary." After a few tugs at his gray beard, "Whatever else I may be, I am a Zionist."

I snagged a few pistachios out of one of the bags. "Would the founders of Zionism be surprised to see the way the country turned out?"

"Oh yes!" Amnon exclaimed. "They wanted a liberal, secular, socialist state. Not surprising the Soviet Union was our first supporter."

Now, Amnon declared, the right had been in power too long, after too many years with the left in power. He was sure that if a deal was made with the Palestinians, with a lessening of external threats, the many splits in Israeli society would become glaring.

"We'll have a showdown between the right and the left. As things are, the high courts are all that stand between secular people like me and the religious right. If worse comes to worst and the right triumphs, I'll withdraw. I won't listen to the radio, the television. I'll be protected in academia. That's what I hope anyway."

I joked, "There should be a country called Academia were academics can seek refuge."

That night, there I was doing something I would have thought inconceivable a short while before, going to bed in the home of a person I hardly knew, in the room of Amnon's daughter. My hands lightly clutching the girlish floral quilt, I listened for sounds that might disturb my sleep. The room faced onto a central court, however, and I didn't hear much of anything. I eyed a squirrel I could make out in a poster pinned to one wall. I imagined it quoting Alan Ladd in *The Blue Dahlia*, after Veronica Lake gives him a lift in her car: "You ought to have more sense than to take chances with strangers like this." To which Veronica and I replied philosophically, "It's funny, but practically all the people I know were strangers when I met them."

The next day, Amnon set off to teach a statistics class wearing the same outfit he had the day before, a blue polo shirt and somewhat worn black corduroys. He did give me a key. Possibly on better acquaintance, he felt comfortable letting me stay in his apartment by myself.

I only went out shortly before Amnon had told me he would return, just to get some exercise. Dear reader, don't expect to find me out roaming at every opportunity in new places I visit. I have two sides, my mother side and my father side, as I frame it. My mother loved to travel. Her greatest pleasure was to be on a trip, her second greatest to plan one. My father, on the other hand, was a dyed-in-the-wool homebody. One of the few ways to arouse his ire was to disturb his routine. Nothing pleased him more than to sit down to dinner at exactly six o'clock. I'm sure he would have preferred a bad dinner at six to a good one at half-past.

Sometimes my mother side is stronger, at other times, my father side. Even within a period of a few days, or a day itself, the balance can shift. My journal during this trip is littered with sentences like, "Didn't go out until three," even "Never left the apartment." I would tend the garden of my emails, read, write in my journal, putter, to the extent I could putter when not in my own home.

After returning from school, Amnon gave me a quick tour of the city center. I offered to take him out to dinner. A kind host, he gave me the choice of eating out or at home. "Either is fine," I said. Still, it wasn't difficult for Amnon to ferret out that I preferred home. One of the chief rules of Couchsurfing is: reward your host. From this point on, I always made sure I arrived with at least one gift in case another chance to reward a host didn't arise.

At the apartment, Amnon pulled out of the refrigerator some mushroom soup he'd made, which was delicious. Then some pasta, which he let me have, getting me to admit I wanted more to eat. A stomach by-pass kept him from eating much at a sitting, he explained.

Upon my arrival, Amnon had invited me to eat anything I wanted in the apartment. It's only fair to warn any future host of mine that there are dangers in this. In India, I'd gotten sick on the food within a week of arriving and afterward never wanted to eat much. In Jordan and Israel, my suppressed appetite came surging back. As I cleaned up after dinner, taking Amnon at his word, I nibbled away. I would take three small cookies from a container, put it back on the shelf, then take it down again and eat a few more. At least I did thoroughly clean the kitchen, put everything away, and close the cupboard doors.

Hanging over my visit was a slight apprehension about the reference Amnon might leave on my Couchsurfing profile. These showed up with a heading of Positive, Negative, or Neutral. Talking with a Dutch guy at my hotel in Amman, we'd agreed that if you got even one negative reference, no one would host you. The only thing you could do was create a new profile and start over. Before I departed the following afternoon, I asked Amnon if he would write me a reference. He gave the impression he hadn't thought of doing this, but said, "Of course."

"Unless it's negative," I smiled, "in which case don't bother."

GERSHEM AND ZELIK

Wheeling my suitcase away from Amnon's building, I felt my first Couchsurfing experience had gone pretty well. The bargain-hunter in me had relished the free lodging. The side of me that craved connection with people had been gratified. On the other hand, the side of me that was "afraid of intimacy," as my partner had complained to our couples counselor, hadn't been overly disturbed. As good as his word, Amnon had left me a reference that, far from being negative, was extremely kind. "From the first minute," he wrote, "it was as if I was hosting an old friend."

A thunder shower broke during my bus ride toward the center of town. One hand on my suitcase, the other clutching my collapsible umbrella, I scurried through the rain to the home of my second host. Hosts rather, since this time I was working the homo angle and staying with a male-male couple.

Gershem and Zelik were in their late twenties; nearer the age of the classic Couchsurfer, though at least with college well behind them. If they were aware of the age difference between us, they were too polite to draw attention to it. The two men shared male pattern baldness that they dealt with in the same way, by means of the short short haircut that had become so nearly universal that I worried hair on men's heads might be making its evolutionary swan song (they told me they cut each other's hair at home). From the hair, they diverged. Zelik taller and a bit heavier, wearing glasses. Gershem's nice white teeth his most notable feature. In a message, Gershem had claimed that Zelik's English was better. Talking to them, I wasn't sure about this, their English seeming equally good.

I offered to take the guys out to dinner, determined to reward my hosts better on this stay. Out of several restaurants they proposed, I chose one that Gershem said made good salads. "Israel has great food," he said. "Much better than the food I had last year on a business trip to Minneapolis." Letting this slur on American cuisine go unchallenged, I ordered a chicken salad. This was indeed delicious, the sort of food I'd been craving after India and Jordan, where I'd avoided leafy greens. Another novelty was to have a waitress instead of a waiter. A third was to be able to ask for tap water and drink it with confidence in its safety.

I asked the two men how they'd met. As a single person, I was a sort of census taker about how people had met their partners, hoping to figure out how to increase my own chances of success.

"A mutual friend invited us both to a party," Zelik said. "At the last minute, no one else could come, and we ended up being the only guests besides our friend."

"Sounds like destiny," I said.

Gershem and Zelik had married a year ago in Vancouver. "Gay people can't marry in Israel," Zelik explained, "but at least the authorities will register a marriage that takes place in another country."

"A Jew and a non-Jew can't marry here either," Gershem said. "The religious right always makes a deal with the other ruling party that they'll control the Ministry of Internal Affairs, which regulates marriage. So we have these crazy rules. For example, that people with the last name Cohen can't marry someone who has been divorced. That's because they're descendants of high priests from before the Diaspora, over two thousand years ago."

Zelik said his generation questioned everything about the country. Thinking of Amnon, I asked what seemed like the most basic question, if he thought Israel should never have been founded in the first place.

"Sometimes I think no, it shouldn't," he said. "Not here anyway. The Zionists went wrong from the point they settled on Palestine as the location. Uruguay would have been a better choice."

"What right did we have to come here?" Gershem said. "I can understand how the Arabs say we're colonists."

I asked Gershem and Zelik where their families were from. Gershem's from Romania; Zelik's from Poland. "Coming from

Poland is considered more prestigious among Israelis," Gershem said. Smiling, "I married well." They'd considered getting
passports from their ancestral homes. The threats that would
make them take this step came both from without (Iran) and
from within (if the religious right gained too much power).
When I asked if the recent Arab Spring uprisings made Israelis
nervous, Gershem replied, "Everything makes Israelis nervous."

In my second surf, I was demoted from sleeping in a bed
in a private room to sleeping on the living room floor. Demoted, or to look at it differently, given a chance to develop
greater adaptability. A Couchsurfer was trustworthy, helpful,
friendly, courteous, cheerful, clean, reverent, and above all
adaptable. I played around with the materials the guys gave
me. If I used one pad, it didn't provide enough cushioning;
if two, the top pad slid against the bottom one, making me
twist this way and that. The best solution I could find was to
wrap the big blanket around me several times, then drop onto
a single pad like a mummy.

Still feeling very new to Couchsurfing, I'd asked Gershem
and Zelik earlier if other surfers had done things that bothered
them. Neither could think of anything. All the same, I tried
to watch my step. In the morning, instead of leaving the pads
out, I returned them to the room the guys used as an office
and folded up the bedding. I put my belongings out on the
enclosed porch and even then kept them in as small a space as
possible. I washed the sink full of dishes.

With Gershem heading off to a class, Zelik and I had the
"Israeli breakfast" offered at a nearby restaurant. This included
a tomato and cucumber salad, dishes of goat cheese cubes and
tuna and other things to spread on bread. Really, too much
food for breakfast. I'd thought Zelik would be a little easier to
spend time with than Gershem, that he would be my favorite

of the two. This was partly based on an impression that he was more outgoing. On closer acquaintance, I wondered if in fact both these guys were on the low-key side. A couple in which like attracts like rather than opposites. Zelik always seemed a little far away from me. Seeing his eyes through his glasses added to this sense of removal.

Before heading off to explore the city, I collected some bits of personal trash in a small bag. I deposited this in a public trash container in the street, not wanting to add anything to my hosts' garbage. I did my best to follow a Leave No Trace plan, treating their home like a nature reserve.

So far, Tel Aviv had made a good impression. Mainly, after India and Amman, that it was similar to a Western city, with street trees, people on bicycles, people walking dogs, women in short skirts, men in T-shirts (only now did I realize the men in Amman almost never wore shirts that exposed their arms). Where was the nearest city like it, in Italy, in Spain? Or did you have to travel as far away as the U.S. to find something truly similar? Having American English be the language I overheard most on the streets after Hebrew emphasized the city's Yankee Doodle quality.

The more I explored Tel Aviv, the more I saw past the window dressing of pretty greenery and jazzy street-level stores, to buildings that looked hastily thrown up, using cheap materials. My philosemitism got me into trouble because I expected Jewish people to be smart and get things right. I assumed everything in a country composed mostly of Jews would be well done; had a hazy vision of Tel Aviv as a near-perfect modern city, which of course it wasn't. Mixed in with my experience of the city were moments of feeling it a privilege to be here. I thought of Jordanians and Palestinians I'd met in Amman who were pretty thoroughly barred from admission.

I returned to the apartment to find Zelik had left to attend a bachelor party in his home town. Gershem and I made a salad using food I'd bought. As with Zelik, we seemed too much the muted, self-conscious types for our pairing to work well. I sensed at times that we both had to push ourselves a little to keep up a conversation. Some of Gershem's hesitancy might have stemmed from uncertainty about his English. A couple of times in the conversation, he gave up on trying to say something because of difficulties with the language.

The night before, I'd asked the guys if they'd considered having children. Gershem had replied that he wanted them and Zelik didn't. As we ate dinner, Gershem told me it wasn't simply that Zelik didn't want children. "He doesn't want to have them in Israel, because he isn't sure they'd have a good future here. Or any future."

Gershem appeared interested in what I had to say about Jews in America. For example, how they'd had a large presence in the early film industry, yet before the Fifties, seldom used their Jewishness as subject matter in their work. I was thankful that like me, he wasn't a fan of Woody Allen.

Gershem asked about the pro-Israeli lobbies in the U.S. "Is it true they have a lot of power?" I told him what little I knew. His next question: "Do Jews control the world?" He lowered his voice, as if doubtful about even asking such a question.

"Are you talking about some crazy idea of a small group of Jewish people running the show behind the scenes?" I said. Gershem didn't reply. Perhaps the language barrier rose again. Had a drop of venom found its way into one of the victims of this kind of propaganda, so that for an instant he questioned if there could possibly be some truth to it; some truth that I, an outsider, might be able to reveal?

The next evening, Gershem and Zelik invited me to see a movie with them at the Cinematique. This was *Gainsbourg (Vie héroïque)*, about Serge Gainsbourg, a French pop singer of the post-war era whom I, in my serious music cocoon, had never heard of before. As we left the theater, Zelik asked if I'd enjoyed the film. Like an overeager child on the Fourth of July, I launched several rockets in quick succession. Could you get secondhand smoke damage from watching a movie with lots of cigarette smoking? (At least one cigarette was lit or getting lit in every scene.) Couldn't we have seen our hero fail to get at least one gorgeous babe into bed? (Instead, one after another – including Brigitte Bardot – succumbed to his charms.) Didn't this film have the same problem as all biopics of way too much territory to cover, unless the subject died young? (The story trundled on until Gainsbourg died at sixty-three, finally done in by an excess of everything).

After each rocket launching, I waited to see which points of mine Zelik would dispute or affirm. He was Jewish, after all, and it was my Jewish friends back in the U.S. who could usually be relied on for a lively debate. Instead, he didn't say anything much, except, eventually, "Well, *I* liked the movie."

I worried I'd offended him, that he thought I was sorry I'd come, which I wasn't. I looked over at Gershem. "What did you think of it?"

Shrug. "Oh, I thought it was pretty good." Nothing more.

I gave up.

Back at the apartment, things improved. While I watched from the couch, the guys practiced a little dance they were supposed to perform at the wedding ceremony of Zelik's friend, preceding the entrance of the bride and groom. Seeing them do their goofy steps, giggling together, Gershem's white teeth flashing and Zelik's glasses twinkling, I wondered if it was their age that created difficulties for me. A feeling of youthful hesitancy in them at times, and a flickering in and out of a conversational mode. I read bad things into these qualities, that people didn't like me.

After Gershem and Zelik went to bed, I tried to make myself comfortable on the living room floor again. Mixed success with this, accompanied by the feeling that as a whole, my second surf had shared this quality.

Chapter 2

Israel: On to Jerusalem

BOAZ AND ILANA

I have a confession to make: I'm not by nature the most punctual person in the world. Some of my worst fights with my ex were over my being late, since he, by contrast, was almost pathologically on time. Post break-up, I was eager to prove I could reform. This led to my reaching Jerusalem the Golden with two hours to kill before I was due at the home of my next host.

Saddled with suitcase and shoulder bag, I sat on a bench in a plaza reading *The Jewel in the Crown*, a novel about India I enjoyed more than experiencing that country in person. The area around the bus station not the best introduction to Jerusalem, with busy roads and big institutional buildings like the Central Zionist Archives. The only thing worth prolonged scrutiny were the many ultra-Orthodox Haredi. The men had scraggly beards and long curling side-locks. They wore long black coats and fedoras that sometimes verged on the stylish, though placed awkwardly high on their heads. As for the women, with their black hose and skirts that came below the knees, stylishness was remote. The Haredi regarded me with reserve, a little suspicious. I had to work to remind myself that all this was "interesting," the sort of thing I'd traveled here to see. Gershem had offered me a Panama hat another Couchsurfer had left behind. Seeing the shadow of this hat on the ground, it looked like that of a fedora. At least my shadow fit in.

Finally climbing onto a local bus, I asked the driver to tell me when we reached a certain stop. I spoke to him in English. His minimal reply was in Hebrew, "*Ken*," yes. Not trusting him to remember, I asked the woman I sat next to if she spoke English. She shook her head. However, the woman in front of her, overhearing, asked if she could help. It only takes one person doing something nice like this to make a sufficient brightness in my experience of a place.

My hosts were Boaz and Ilana. Boaz was a beefy guy whose nose seemed perpetually stuffed up, making him breathe through his mouth. This gave his talk an air of the childish, though also the endearing. Ilana, too, was ample; plain, though with a self-assurance that made me soon forget this. I couldn't be too critical of the love of food their physiques made obvious, since this soon produced a tasty dinner of rice, baked salmon, and tabbouleh. I was still in a hungry phase and particularly enjoyed the rice, combining each bite with some tahini. That Boaz and Ilana ate with much gusto gave me permission to do the same. For all three of us, the answer to "Would you like some more?" was invariably, "Yes!"

More talk about Israel. First, about the tension between the Ashkenazi and Sephardi Jews. "Another division in the country!" I exclaimed, adding this to the mental list I'd been compiling: the left versus the right, the Haredi versus the secularists, the Russians versus the Europeans. "How many can there be?"

Then about the Haredi. "They'll take over a building," Boaz said in his stuffed-up voice. "First have a middleman buy an apartment, and soon the neighbors find a Haredi family moving in. Sometimes the families will buy several apartments and all move in on the same day."

"They keep trying to impose their standards," Ilana said. "Ask if you can not play your television or stereo so loudly on Shabbat, things like that. Two men knocked on our door one day and told me people in the neighborhood thought I should dress more modestly."

"What did you say?" I asked.

She threw up her hands. "What can you say to people like that? Nothing. I just closed the door."

Ilana told me she was politically more on the left than Boaz. "And you're in the center?" I asked him.

"No," Boaz said, "the idea of the center is a myth. There is no center. Either you're on the left or the right."

Later in the conversation, Boaz said, "You know what Israel really should do – which it never will? Break off its friendship with the United States and do what's in its best interests. Say to the Palestinians that Israel isn't going to give up Jerusalem or the settlements in the West Bank, that they can have an independent country with what's left if they want, all broken up, like the original proposal for Israel."

As I'd found talking with other Israelis, Boaz and Ilana appeared willing to tell me their most private thoughts about the country. Often before I could ask some provocative question, they'd already voiced it themselves. A disarming habit.

I was sleeping in a back room used for storage. The bed was already made, and in a welcoming touch, a bath towel and a hand towel were folded on the duvet. The couple left the door to their room open, and I could hear Boaz snore. I tried to see this as pleasantly familial.

Ilana had left by the time I got up, and Boaz was just about to go. I went out in the afternoon. Before getting on a bus, I took a close look at the surroundings of the stop to ensure I would recognize them when I returned. One of the many differences between Couchsurfing and conventional travel was that my lodgings weren't picked out with a convenient sign saying "Hilton" or "Hippie Dippie Hostel." Nor could I get a taxi there or ask for directions by using the name. I was making this trip before the average mobile phone had blossomed into a Swiss Army knife of features. The one I had with me functioned for calls and texts, which at the time seemed like miracle enough. I therefore needed to know the exact address of my host and to take some mental photographs so I could remember things like the nearest bus stop. In a later chapter, I'll show what happens when I fail to follow these rules.

I got off the bus at a point Ilana had indicated on a map she'd printed for me and walked toward the walled city. The older buildings I passed were constructed of blocks of pale stone, while the new buildings were faced with it, as required by local regulations. The effect was harmonious, though rather bland. I wasn't sure if plain pale stone was the best building material for an entire city.

It gave me a touristic thrill to spot the ancient city walls. Running parallel to these, farther down the slope, stood a mall. It was upscale, tasteful, and with the usual expensive stone facing, but still, a mall. Looking around, I saw that all the black-costumed figures had vanished except for one man who was running, as if to escape these fleshpots.

I entered the walled city through the Jaffa Gate. Absent in the mall, the Haredi predominated in the Jewish Quarter. They hurried past me and the other tourists as if on urgent business. Toward evening, I came to the Western Wall, seeing it down below and across a plaza. After passing through security, I walked into the section for women by mistake – the women were allotted a stretch of the Wall only about a quarter as long as the men. After hurrying back out, I observed the scene close to the Wall from behind a metal barrier that came up to my chin. Jerusalem was at a higher elevation than Tel Aviv, and it was cold in March and grew colder as twilight came on. The wind blew off the white kippas some men had donned to approach the Wall. Swallows skimmed about, sometimes inserting themselves with incredible neatness into the higher crevices.

Passing through another security point on the opposite side of the plaza, I found myself entering the Muslim Quarter. I felt uneasy here, inevitably aligning myself with the Jews while at the same time having a moment of thinking it was nice to hear Arabic again, as in Amman. A slender crescent moon lay on its back in the sky, echoing the moon atop a minaret. Having gone quite far in one direction, I returned the way I'd come in an almost straight line, not wanting to get lost.

I'd offered to take Boaz and Ilana out to dinner. Later, they sent me a text saying they preferred to eat at home. This didn't surprise me. They were eaters, and one could eat so much better at home if one cooked as well as Ilana. I bought some groceries on the way back. Seeing these, Ilana exclaimed, "You're crazy! We already have plenty of food." She prepared a tasty spaghetti dish and used some of the things I'd bought in a green salad. She'd already made tiramisu for dessert, "since she was bored," as Boaz explained. "She makes desserts whenever she'd bored." "In that case," I smiled, "I'm glad she was bored today."

With Gershem and Zelik, conversation was a seasonal stream, sometimes flowing, sometimes not. With Boaz and Ilana, there was always a flow. Boaz made us laugh, telling stories about his mother. "She was always after me to achieve, achieve. Once I achieved one thing, she was telling me to achieve something else. First to get a good job, then to marry. I want to know what she's going to tell me to achieve when I'm on my death bed."

Getting up after Boaz and Ilana had left in the morning, I found one or both had consumed almost the entire package of chocolate chip cookies I'd brought home yesterday, not knowing Ilana had made dessert; this, after we'd all had two servings of her tiramisu. Moreover, I noticed that the serving spoon for the tiramisu, which I'd washed the night before, was back in the sink, showing someone had eaten more either last night or in the morning.

Letting a Couchsurfer into your home could be like letting in Sherlock Holmes.

CARL

In his profile, my next host, Carl, said he lived in Ein Karem, which was on the western edge of the city. When I told Boaz and Ilana this was where I would be staying, they exclaimed that Ein Karem was one of their favorite parts of Jerusalem, near lots of places for countryside walks. I congratulated myself on my wise choice. However, before reaching its last stop, where my host had told me to get off, the bus passed through the village of Ein Karem, continued a long way downhill, and finally entered the grounds of what was signed as an Agricultural School. Later, Carl explained that for the last ten years, these facilities had been used as a boarding school for children from troubled families, whom he taught. Families would have difficulty troubling any child tucked away in this remote location, with olive orchards on the side closer to the city and pine forests on the other. While I liked having access to the countryside, I wasn't sure I wanted to spend several nights completely submerged in it.

I called Carl from the bus stop to say I'd arrived. "I forgot you were coming," he admitted. "I'm driving back to the school. I should be there in fifteen minutes."

"That's fine," I said, thinking this visit wasn't starting well.

Carl went on to say he had other surfers staying with him, something he hadn't told me before. At first I thought he said two Russians. "Two?" I questioned. "No, three," he replied. Okay, *three* Russians. A Couchsurfer is above all adaptable.

Carl had been shopping for groceries. After installing me in his modest, messy house, he left almost at once, needing to teach a class. Carl hadn't brought in the groceries from the car, and his invitation to eat anything I wanted was rendered rather meaningless by the Mother Hubbard condition of the cupboards. Thinking I could buy things here, I'd only brought along some apples, oranges, and rye crackers. I did find a jar of honey and another of tahini, and spread both on my crackers. Munching on these, I fantasized about what Boaz and Ilana might be having for dinner that night.

Carl had told me I could walk back to Ein Karem and pointed out the general direction in which it lay. As he'd suggested, I asked the guard at the front gate for specifics. Unfortunately the guard didn't speak English. He tried to find a ride for me among several cars leaving, then to get me on a

41

bus. Finally I had a woman who was passing explain to him that I didn't want to ride to the village, I wanted to know how to *walk* there. Walking any distance has perhaps become an incomprehensible act in the modern world.

To get off the busy road as it zigzagged up toward Ein Karem, I made my way through olive groves planted on a series of rough terraces. In the village, I found tourists, restaurants, and a couple of churches of no great interest. I ate a slice of pizza and bought what food I could find at a very small store, almonds, tomatoes, bananas, cookies. Then, not wanting to get caught out after dark, I hurried down a dirt road that led more directly back toward the school than the route I'd taken coming up. I felt a little adventurous, though I wasn't covering great distances and the hilly terrain gave me plenty of chances to get my bearings.

Carl's solution to the key-for-guests issue was simple: he left his front door unlocked. This made sense in a location that was remote, fenced, and had a guard at the entrance. No one there when I entered. Carl had told me he wouldn't get back until eleven-thirty, while I had no idea when the Russians would arrive.

Finally at ten the Russians showed up. To my relief, they seemed like sweet, well-behaved young men. They all had similar names, Alexander, Alexei, and some other variant. Alexander and Alexei were brothers, only two years apart and with different hair styles that at first kept me from seeing the family resemblance in other features. Alexander's hair was straight and longish, Alexei's dark and curly. Both had smooth skin of amazing paleness. I associated this with their having been raised in Murmansk, which they said was the most northerly major city in the world, though they lived in Moscow at present.

Alexander, who spoke the best English, also talked by far the most. I assumed the ability and the volubility went hand in hand. Alexei made hesitant attempts. He often asked Alexander a word or phrase, which made his brother impatient. Their skinny friend spoke some English when nudged by the others, though was mainly silent.

Alexander kept up an extended conversation with me. However, I remember more about Alexei's talk, either because he was cuter or because having to fill in words for him involved me more. He was reading a Jack London novel. Encouraged by Alexander, he outlined the plot. "The bad men, they" (word consultation with his brother) "steal the dog that he is in California, and they put him into a" (consultation) "ship and take him to the north to Alaska, and they make him to pull a" (consultation) "sled in the" (consultation) "snow."

I told the Russians I wanted to visit their country because I'd heard that in the cities, there were lots of intellectuals. I'm not sure they understood this. Nothing for us to do except keep talking until Carl arrived, as he did at last.

The brothers slept on a mattress placed on the living room floor, while the friend and I occupied two matching yellow couches. The couch cushions were thin and had only a board under them. My back hurt as the night progressed. Still, I saw myself as advancing higher in the School of Couchsurfing, going from sleeping in a private room in the home of a stranger (Amnon), to a living room in the home of strangers (Gershem and Zelik), to sharing my sleeping space with strangers.

Waking before the others, I sat on the couch reading, hemmed in by the mattress, which took up most of the floor. Later the Russians joined me in reading, the skinny friend using an e-reader.

The last of us to get up was Carl, at around ten. Carl had some dark handsomeness that was getting buried under fat as he aged. Puttering about in a sleeveless T-shirt, putting one or both arms behind his head so that his underarms were displayed, the heavy, earthy side of him was more evident than yesterday.

In Israel, Carl told me, teaching was a lousy job. "People here would rather do any other kind of work." He was thinking about immigrating to Germany, to Leipzig perhaps. He had a Czech grandfather who should make this possible. Yet another Israeli with an escape plan.

Carl was a sculptor. His house was dotted with various small statues he'd made, of a head, a hand. Most were of white plaster that was gathering a patina of dust. "I want to get more serious about my sculpting," he said. "Maybe I can become an itinerant sculptor, moving from city to city as I work on different commissions." This struck me as wishful thinking, as do most people's notions about having an artistic career, including my own.

Carl made *shakshuka*, with me cutting up onions and garlic while Alexei – shoved into the kitchen by the other two, perhaps because he had some cooking skills – juiced some oranges and pomegranates. Later, a friend of Carl's, Doron, arrived to help organize a movie he would make with the kids at the school's Purim Party. Doron was tall, with black hair cut in short bangs, dark hair on his arms. As some people's expressiveness was in their eyes, so Doron's was in his eloquent black eyebrows. Up they shot to show surprise or amusement, down they came for puzzlement, disapproval. They even had that rare ability to angle up in the middle, which he used to convey quizzicalness. While Carl was telling us a story, Doron assumed yoga poses. "Do you know the theater phrase 'stealing focus'?" I teased him. "That's what you're doing."

Doron had brought along a collection of hats for the party. We tried them on, laughing. Bonnet, sombrero, cowboy hat, fireman helmet, aviator cap with ear flaps, a red turban. Doron took a photograph of the five of us, telling us to crowd together on one of the couches and, of course, give a big smile. Someone seeing the resulting photograph might wish he'd been there with us, we looked as if we were having so much fun. In fact like most posed photographs, it captured a partly invented moment, with Alexander putting an arm around my shoulders that he immediately removed afterward. We were having *some* fun, not a lot.

Carl went off to spend time with a group of kids as a residential manager, a sort of den mother, while the Russians headed toward the bus stop to go into town. I accompanied them to the stop, then returned to the house, deciding it was too cold, I wouldn't enjoy myself. I washed the dishes, without soap, since I found there wasn't any, and went for another country ramble.

When the Russians came back in the evening, for some reason Alexander was no longer talkative with me. We all read. Alexei, having finished his novel, browsed through Carl's collection of art books. Carl returned. I was disappointed he didn't thank me for doing the dishes or apparently even notice they'd been cleaned. Maybe in the same way that he wasn't aware of the dirt and chaos in his house, he wasn't aware when these were reduced. At nine-thirty, later than I myself would have wanted to go out, he and the Russians took off to have a drink somewhere. I went to bed early, hoping to catch up on the sleep I'd missed the night before. I'd had the Russians put out the mattress, which helped minimize their disturbing me when they came back at around midnight.

The brothers had a giggly whispered conversation early in the morning, after which they returned to sleep while I could not. They may have disturbed my shut-eye, but they also gave me some cultural food for thought. These two were physically affectionate in a way most American brothers or friends would almost never be. The day before while they read, Alexander rested his arm on Alexei's shoulder. Later this morning, they almost cuddled in their red sleeping bags.

It rained off and on, sometimes quite hard. Carl made an early lunch, saying he felt like cooking. A curry with tomatoes and onions, though no rice or bread to accompany it. I shared my rye crackers, along with some cut up apples. I wished the Russians had brought food with them at some point, and also that they would wash the dishes this time. However, I could keep a slight distance from these thoughts. Who knows, maybe in Russia, guests never bought groceries or cleaned the dishes.

Carl offered to drive us to the Israel Museum. Again, I got ready to go, then, confronted with the rain, I told him I would rather stay behind if that was all right. "Your place is so cozy," I said. "Whatever you want to do," he said and put his hand to his heart in the Middle Eastern gesture of sincerity and respect. I pondered what Carl was getting out of having us here, three young Russians and a middle-aged American. He might just be showing the "true Couchsurfing spirit" discussed on the website. I was glad I didn't go out since the sporadic rain continued.

Carl created a pirate costume for the party that evening. "I'm good at costumes," he said. I doubted he had much to work with in this bare little house. To my surprise, he came into the living room wearing a fair approximation of a pirate costume. He'd wound a dark T-shirt over one eye to suggest an eye patch, a long-sleeved one around his head to create a sort of sailor's head scarf. He took the cowboy hat Doron had left and pinned it into a three-cornered pirate hat. He used tin foil to create a silver tooth. In and out of the room he went, puttering, scrounging, asking my opinion of what he'd done, what else a pirate would wear.

Carl set off for the party. Later the Russians returned, coming in from the wet and cold. They'd brought some pita bread, that was all, and they ate most of that themselves. They offered it to Carl when he appeared, but not to me, though in any case I wouldn't have wanted it. In the same way that I didn't want Indian food in India almost as soon as I arrived there, in Israel I took an instant dislike to the ubiquitous pita bread. The Russians still hardly talked to me. Alexander gave short answers when I asked how their day had been, where they'd gone. Rather than announcing they were going to bed, the brothers just got out the mattress, and all three climbed into their sleeping bags. At a younger age, I would have felt I must figure out why these guys had cooled toward me, worrying I might have offended them in some way. Older, I realized I could pick my figuring-out battles. This was one I decided to forgo.

In the morning, I sat using my laptop at the kitchen table with my back to the others while the Russians took their leave of Carl. Carl told them how to find him on Facebook. "See you in Russia!" they cried. I just smiled and said goodbye, turning to them as they passed through the door.

PAVEL

Late in the afternoon, Carl was nice enough to drive me to the home of my new host, sparing me a long bus ride back into downtown and out again. We curved around the edge of Jerusalem to Mevaseret Zion, which turned out to be almost as far from the center as the Agricultural School. At least it was a real neighborhood, with houses and apartment buildings, all relentlessly surfaced in Jerusalem stone.

Continuing the Russian theme, my host was Pavel, originally from Nizhny Novgorod. Pavel was tall, with what I thought of as a typically Russian face, mainly thanks to something about the cheek bones, maybe a general Asiatic flatness.

Pavel responded to my questions, yet our conversation never caught fire; and though his English was good, listening to his slow, whispery voice with its thick Russian accent, I could tell speaking it required some effort from him. His main job was designing an events calendar website for a start-up company. I assumed there must be many such sites, but couldn't get at what was going to make his stand out from the competitors. Pavel also had a part-time job teaching martial arts, and he talked a little about that. Pavel was well-meaning, doing his best to be a good host, which counted for a lot. While being a good host didn't extend to offering me anything to eat (he'd just eaten himself), I'd brought along cereal, milk, and yogurt, and I made a meal out of this. I was Pavel's very first Couchsurfing guest, which might have explained his rather uncertain hosting manner.

I worried this was going to be a difficult visit. Not because of anything bad about any particular moment, but because of the large number of moments that would be laid end to end. The next day was Shabbat, which meant no bus service between sunset today and sunset tomorrow. During that time, I was pretty much trapped in this outlying neighborhood.

The rest of Friday passed at a slow pace, which grew even slower on Saturday. I spent a lot of time looking for new hosts in Tel Aviv, until my neck hurt from my position sitting on the couch and typing on the coffee table. Sometimes Pavel used the computer in his room; at other times he sat in a bean bag chair in front of the television playing video games. He was right in my line of vision, his back to me.

I could usually tune out the games. Sometimes I watched them, curious to see what their appeal was. Or rather, how the appeal could last for more than a few minutes. Superficially different, the games seemed in essence the same. Pavel would storm into some house or other location and blow away as many of the enemy as possible when they appeared. It wasn't clear to me if it was ever possible for the enemy to blow *him* away, which made the male bravado of the game appear spurious. Although Pavel told me he was trying not to spend too much time playing these games, as the day went on, he racked up quite a bit. I felt guilty for being a witness to his high usage, even a silent one. I did my laundry, using the washing machine in the kitchen. It was one of those European ones that in the eyes of an American did a small amount of wash in an extraordinarily long amount of time. This was one modest achievement of the day, though in violation of Shabbat rules. I expected a man in a long black coat and fedora to burst in and issue me a citation.

I only left the apartment once late in the afternoon, and Pavel never went out at all. The world looked bleak on my walk, the sun trying to drill a hole through the clouds. No children in the several playgrounds. Only a few cars on the streets. It was as if a large part of the population had been killed off or gone into hiding. I reached some commercial establishments, Cup O Joe's, a sushi restaurant, both closed. Farther on, a deserted shopping center, the silver carts fitted together in a row. A McDonald's, identified in Hebrew, with timidly small golden arches.

Was it interesting to see what an ordinary neighborhood on the outskirts of Jerusalem was like on Shabbat? Somewhat.

All the same, from this point on in my travels, I took more care to find out exactly where a potential host lived in a city and whether there was reliable public transportation.

At six, Pavel's girlfriend Korina arrived. All of a sudden, my visit brightened. Korina used to be a ballet dancer and at present was studying to be an architect. We chatted about architecture, agreeing we weren't crazy about the Bauhaus and its progeny.

"I miss statues on buildings," I said.

"I do, too!" Korina exclaimed.

"And the top of a building looking different from the bottom."

"Yes!"

I found Korina mesmerizing to gaze at, especially after being around mainly dark-haired, brown-eyed people for so long, first Indians, then Jordanians, then Israelis. She had blonde hair, gorgeous white skin with pink tints stronger here, lighter there, and contrastingly dark gray eyes with dark lashes.

I could tell by the way Pavel looked at Korina and touched her that he was completely smitten with her. He couldn't be the sort of outgoing person she was (nor could I, for that matter), yet at least he appreciated her. I wove a fantasy that she was telling Pavel he shouldn't play video games so much, and that she'd pushed him to sign up for Couchsurfing. "Pavel, my little samovar, I love you," I imagined her saying, "but you've got to come out of your shell."

Korina told me she wasn't Jewish. More particularly, that her father had been Jewish and not her mother. "That makes me a Jew in Russian eyes, though not always in Israeli eyes. Immigration say yes, other authorities no." She told me about working as a waitress for a difficult boss. He'd been Haredi or at least leaned in that direction, and when there was some last straw and Korina quit in a huff, she threw in that she wasn't Jewish. "'Not *Jewish!*'" she exclaimed, imitating the boss, flinging up her hands in horror.

On Sunday, I drove into the city with Pavel and Korina. Pavel dropped Korina at the university. As he took me nearer to the center, he suddenly said some interesting things, such as that Jerusalem had once had a Haredi mayor and his tenure was a disaster. With Korina present, he'd sat back and watched her scintillate. Having just parted from her, he scintillated a bit on his own, as if still under her spell.

At eleven, I went on a tour of the old city. Sometimes I enjoyed tours, sometimes I didn't. This was one of the times I did. A tour was especially useful in a city where I hadn't got a guidebook. Traveling without a guidebook was another experiment on this leg of my journey, in addition to Couchsurfing. In advance of previous trips, I'd always read at least one guidebook from cover to cover. I even brought along photocopied pages from others, because you could never tell what you might want to know while out in the field, such as the exact meaning of that sculpted figure high atop a column in a Gothic cathedral. I probably could have found an English guidebook to Israel in Tel Aviv, but resisted the impulse, wanting to see what it was like to let go of this support. Too often a guidebook set me off on a connect-the-dots trail of sights, or raised my expectations about some building or monument so that I was almost inevitably disappointed by the reality.

The guide, Ari, was one of those American-Israeli mixes who seemed fairly common. He'd spent some time here growing up, some time in the U.S.; was applying for a graduate program at Cal in Comparative Religions. He spoke English with an American accent and was also fluent in Hebrew. The only peculiarity of his English was a habit of saying you *might* see something that you clearly *did*: "Behind me, you may see the tower of the Church of the Ascension." Unless you were blind, of course. I learned some interesting things from Ari, such as that the plants growing on the Western Wall were left there deliberately. This had puzzled early commentators, who conjectured the Jews were praying to them.

With the sun nearing the horizon, I walked all the way to the not-so-central Central Bus Station, where I caught a bus out to Pavel's. After collecting my luggage, I returned to the station. From there, I walked all the way down Jaffa Road to the home of my next hosts, hauling my suitcase. I arrived at their front door tired from all this to-ing and fro-ing and wishing I could say to them, "Hello, it's very nice to meet you, but do you mind if I just sit quietly somewhere and read for an hour or two?"

Sometimes I thought of myself as a flower with petals that now were open, now shut. Couchsurfing was training me to keep them open more, showing me this was possible, even pleasurable. In fact, ten minutes after I'd entered their house, if my hosts had asked if I wanted to sit somewhere and read, I would have said, "No, I'd much rather go on talking with you."

EDAN AND RAZIEL

Edan and Raziel lived in a narrow old house with thick walls. The strangely high vaulted ceiling left room for a sleeping loft above the area where Edan had his desk. I was to sleep in what the couple called the water hole, where water used to be stored. I reached it by descending a ladder, with Edan handing down my suitcase. I could stand upright in the front half of the space, while in the back, I had to stoop slightly.

Edan did computer work that had medical applications. At the moment he was part of a team creating a tiny implant to help people with glaucoma. Raziel taught autistic children and was attending school. They both grew on me, though Raziel had an absent quality, as if her mind were always elsewhere. I was never sure she was enjoying our conversation as much as Edan and I. Edan was sweet and pixie-ish, with a peculiar high voice and laugh. We ate soup Raziel had made, along with some rolls and cookies I'd bought on my walk here. I also gave them an herbal soap from India since they were counter-culture types who would probably enjoy this. I was their first Couchsurfer, as I'd been Pavel's. "I feel such a responsibility," I joked. "If you have a bad experience with me, you may never host again."

My bed was a pad on a platform built against one wall, with white mosquito netting draped around it. This might sound exotic, sleeping in the water hole of an old Jerusalem house. Alas, the netting made me feel oppressed and shut in, and something in the air made me so congested, I got several handkerchiefs wet with sneezing. The couple's cat, Luna, was a possible culprit, though Edan assured me she never came down into the water hole, wary of the ladder. The netting another, since it looked rather old and dusty. How did you clean mosquito netting, after all?

Returning to the walled city the following day, I strayed through the Muslim Quarter. I soon became claustrophobic amid the narrow streets and was glad to emerge at Herod's Gate. I found myself in a different Jerusalem, a shabbier, mainly Arab one. It had the feeling of a parallel universe, some alternate version of the city, differently populated. Farther east, I could see down into the Valley of Jehoshaphat and up to the Mount of Olives, which was more like the Ridge of Olives. I walked up a dirt road through a park planted with olive trees, the light almost painfully bright.

I felt uncomfortable walking along the ridge. Voices were louder here than in the Other Jerusalem, the young men more boisterous. One of them appeared to make a feint toward me with a cart he was pushing. Tour buses plowed up and down the road. Evidently, this was an area tourists visited, but didn't walk through.

At last I reached a point where I could see the walled city on the other side of the valley. The Dome of the Rock dominated, with its blue walls and glistening gold dome. I descended past the Jewish cemeteries on the slope. Ari had told us that Jews believed this was the place where God would start to redeem the dead on Judgment Day, and burial here provided you with the best place in line. Today's excursion the sort that, while it wasn't altogether pleasant at the time, I was glad I'd made after the fact. It gave me a more balanced view of the city.

Raziel was spending the night at an old people's home, another one of her jobs. Edan went off on a run. "So you'll be back in an hour or so?" I said. "Yes," he said. This gave me time to indulge in the solitary vice, down in the water hole. I mention this only because it's a detail usually omitted from people's narratives, so that as a reader I'm left to ask myself, But when and where did he/she . . . ? Or did he/she just never . . . ?

In the morning, I hauled my suitcase up the water hole ladder and set off on the next stage of my journey, heading for . . .

Chapter 3

West Bank, Back to Israel

BASEEM

. . . Ramallah, twenty-five kilometers away. I hadn't originally intended to visit the West Bank. Then I realized that while I was in this part of the world, I should go Through the Looking-Glass. In Amman, I heard Palestinians talk about Israel, which they'd never visited, and in Israel, Israelis talk about the West Bank, which they in turn had never seen, except possibly as a soldier or for a darting visit to some narrowly defined destination. As an outsider to the two cultures, I had the ability to travel in both places. When I asked Israelis if it was safe for me to go to the West Bank, they said they didn't know. This left my fearful self with scope to play, though it could never figure out precisely what it was worried might happen.

In a small parking lot close to the walls of the old city, I got into a *sherut*. By stepping into this shabby van, where a woman sat wearing a hijab, hey presto, I was already on my way to the Muslim world. We were never out in the country-side on the trip, passing through a conurbation that was more or less continuous from East Jerusalem. Soon I had a glimpse of a round watchtower manned by a guard and the West Bank Barrier, made of vertical slabs of concrete. We drove through an entrance in it without any sort of check. The checking occurred as people left, I realized. On the inner side of the wall, there was some graffiti that included the word GHETTO. I pondered how an Israeli would feel about being accused of confining other people in a ghetto.

Ramallah reminded me of Amman. The wisdom of Tel Aviv was to dress up its uninteresting architecture with frills of greenery. Here, I was back to the vegetation-free Arabic urban world. Pictures of Yasser Arafat were displayed in store windows; one shop was called Arafat Sweets. People sometimes stared at me as I trundled along with my suitcase. Desperate for attention as I was, I usually liked this. From the Lion Square, I called Baseem, my host. He'd offered to collect me here since his home was difficult to find.

While I waited, a hearty old man struck up a conversation with me, asking where I was from. He said he'd grown up in Ramallah and explained that the lion sculptures in the center of the square had been made in Italy. I gathered he just wanted to be friendly; maybe also to propagandize a little for the Palestinian cause, or at any rate show a foreigner a welcome that would make him favorably inclined. At least he didn't want to sell me something. That's the one thing I didn't like as a traveler, the friendly chap with the rug shop around the corner.

Baseem arrived in a dark suit. He had a wonderful mass of curly black hair and pop-out brown eyes. Dark rings under his eyes and flecks of moles on his nose detracted somewhat from his good features. As we walked along, Baseem exchanged greetings with people – I should say more specifically, with men. He introduced me to a man standing in front of his shop. The man shook hands with me, smiling pleasantly, and we chatted for a few minutes. I was impressed by what I saw as the sociability and good manners of the people here, as in Amman.

We took a *sherut* to Baseem's apartment. Although spacious, this was almost bare of furniture, as if Baseem had just moved in, though in fact he'd lived here for over a year. I met the other surfers who were staying with Baseem, a young couple from Lyon. Odette and Didier were both journalists who had quit their jobs and set out for India and other places. Mainly they were traveling to see the world, though in addition they sent reports back to the newspaper they'd worked for and sought out places where news was happening, such as Egypt after Mubarak stepped down. Odette was pretty in a gamine way and spoke better English than her husband. We were to sleep on pads on the living room floor. Tonight I would once again be a Padsurfer.

In his profile, Baseem had mentioned being a male belly dancer. As the four of us made dinner, his love of dancing came up.

"As soon as I arrive in a new city, I go out looking for the night life," he said, frying some slices of squash in a pan. "Whenever I go to a dance place, I'll be surrounded by gay men asking me to dance. That's all right. I don't mind gay people. But I don't like it when they approach me by grabbing my crotch."

I wish I could report that I was quick-witted enough to say, with a smile of gentle skepticism, "Are you sure about the crotch grabbing, Baseem? No man has ever grabbed *my* crotch." I wasn't.

As there was almost no furniture in the apartment, so there was almost nothing to eat with. We had difficulty finding glasses for all of us, until Baseem turned up some plastic ones. Since there was only one chair and one stool at the kitchen table, we sat on pads placed by the living room window. Baseem said we could use silverware and individual plates if we liked. Otherwise, we would eat the Arab way, scooping up the chicken bits and squash and other items with the ubiquitous pita bread. We all agreed to go Arab.

While we ate, I questioned Baseem about his work. This was with an organization that gave advice and financing to young Palestinians who wanted to start businesses. In one success story, the organization had bought a young man ten sheep. "A year later, he'd turned ten sheep into twenty," Baseem said proudly.

Baseem also volunteered with One Voice, a group trying to push forward the settlement process. "The group has an Israeli branch and a Palestinian one, though the two don't interact much aside from meeting a few times each year. Instead, they work parallel to one another. The group sees the two state solution as the only realistic possibility."

I brought up the Israeli settlements in the West Bank. "Why is Israel so determined to have them?"

Baseem had the answer – he was the type who had all the answers. "The settlements are part of a strategy. If the Israelis agree to abandon them in negotiations, we Palestinians will think we've scored a great victory. That will distract from the important things we aren't getting, like control of our borders and the right to have an army."

I asked Baseem if he thought the Second Intifada had been a mistake. Yes, he said, a big mistake, a huge miscalculation. He claimed Israel was behind it. "Israel wanted an excuse to clamp down on us and build the Wall. Sharon provoked us by visiting the Temple Mount surrounded by hundreds of Israeli riot police. Israel manipulated Arafat into starting the Intifada." Keyed-up, Baseem swept both hands back through his mass of black curls. "The Israelis are very clever."

This struck me as the cliche of the sly, clever Jew. At times, Baseem even voiced what he saw as the sentiments of the Israelis in a stereotypical, whining "Jewish" voice. The more I listened to Baseem, the less he appeared the reasonable, pragmatic sort of person he wished to portray himself as, with his "non-violent grass roots organization."

"You seem to see Israel as a monolith," I said. "My impression is that Israeli society is actually very divided." Baseem didn't give any sign of hearing me.

What Baseem had said about Palestine wanting an army caught in my mind. I said, "You say you advocate the two state solution, but what about after it's achieved? Do you have a plan for something else later on?"

Baseem smiled, looking pleased. "I'm not saying anything."

I made a guess. "You remind me of Ben-Gurion saying when he agreed to the U.N. partition plan that this was only the first step."

"The Palestinians should learn from the Israelis," Baseem said. Again, that strange mix of hating the Israelis and admiring them, and thinking they were so clever and so united. His implication seemed clear, that once Palestine had control over its own territory, it would create an army, attack Israel, and regain the whole country.

While I wasn't sure exactly what the journalistic style of the French couple was, it certainly didn't seem to involve going for the jugular. Didier said not a word throughout this conversation, Odette just a little. Both attentive, as if we were at a lecture, which in a sense we were. I asked myself whether Baseem was using Couchsurfing to spread the Palestinian word to receptive young people.

Odette used to be a dancer, and at her suggestion, we attended a modern dance performance at a theater in the center of Ramallah. The most interesting thing to me was how pseudo-Tel Aviv the event was; that is to say, how Western. The theater, its small lobby with a chandelier and a marble floor; the audience, in which I saw only a few women wearing the hijab; the arty, plotless dances; the pleasant hubbub afterward as people stood chatting on the street in front of the theater.

Off to a cafe, La Vie. This, too, was completely Tel Avivian. It had a pretty terrace with plants in containers, outdoor tables lit by candles. There was even a blonde waitress who spoke what I thought was American English, though she revealed she was Danish. I recognized people from the theater, though the theater and cafe weren't very close to each other. Perhaps there were only a limited number of places like this to frequent in the city.

More talk about the Israel-Palestine conundrum. "Young Israelis are brain-washed," Baseem said. "They just repeat what they're told by the authorities." The Palestinians struck me as even more brainwashed. However, I kept this thought to myself.

Maybe it was my glass of Palestinian wine, but suddenly I felt I had a useful insight, that Palestinians and Israelis had many similarities. "They both often have international connections. Like many Palestinians, lots of Israelis have had the experience of being refugees. Why can't the two groups emphasize their common points instead of their differences?" Again, Baseem didn't respond, as if he hadn't heard what I said. It wasn't part of the standard script.

Pita bread and hummus for breakfast in the morning. I felt it would be a long time before I wanted to eat either of these foods again after leaving the Middle East.

GRETA

That morning, I took a *sherut* to Bethlehem. Signs indicated the road we traveled on was a gift from the American people to the Palestinian people. The only moment to grab my attention in the dance performance last night had been when a box labeled "U.S. Aid" was thrown onto the stage, making the audience laugh. I was less amused myself to reflect that, through American foreign aid, I helped provide the equivalent of around five hundred dollars a year to every Israeli citizen and I didn't know how much to every Palestinian.

Arriving at Oh Little Town Of, I called my hostess Greta on my mobile. I felt put off by her at once. Determining exactly where I was in the town, telling me not to take a taxi, giving me directions to her place on foot, she sounded impatient, abrasive. After reaching the street she lived on, I couldn't find her building number and had to call again. More impatience that I hadn't remembered her saying that at the top of the public stairs, I continued straight through a gate. Once I arrived, yet more impatience when I didn't at once grasp her instructions about how to close an inner door of her apartment on the way out.

I was tempted to say to Greta, "I don't like you, I don't feel comfortable staying with you, I'm going to check into a hotel." Yet was she truly so provoking that I had to take this step? No, I kept deciding, from one moment to the next. I saw that another quality needed to be added to the Couchsurfing Law: I shall be trustworthy, helpful, friendly, courteous, cheerful, clean, reverent, adaptable – and tolerant, avoiding snap judgments. As we continued to talk, I just behaved as if I were comfortable with Greta. I teased her about something, used her name. This actually did make our interaction more pleasant.

Greta's small building was one of a half-dozen facing a communal terrace. We sat here in the shade of some trees drinking tea. Greta was early forties, German, dark, pretty-ish. She'd spent four years teaching at several schools in Bethlehem, mainly the German language. She contrasted her often lazy, unmotivated students here with the hardworking Taiwanese she'd taught earlier. Recently she'd told one of her better Palestinian students that she could apply for a four month stay in Germany, with all expenses paid. The girl told her she couldn't leave at the required time because she needed to attend a family wedding. "There are family weddings every day in Palestine!" Greta exclaimed to me. Most of the smarter, more ambitious Palestinians had emigrated, she said, leaving the more hidebound ones behind.

The Palestinians blamed the Israelis for all their problems, according to Greta. "Every day at school begins with the announcement of how many Palestinians have been killed by Israelis at the checkpoints and elsewhere. *Every single day.*" At one of the schools, the children were taught in German to a German curriculum. This included material on the Holocaust. Some students had expressed approval at the idea of Jews getting killed. "When students complained I was spending too much time on this subject, my boss, who's a priest, told me not to discuss 'politics' in the classroom. I suppose 'politics' includes presenting the Holocaust as a reason to feel sympathetic toward Jews."

I offered to take Greta out to dinner. She said, "I can't go out because I called in sick today – I already told you." This was another one of her abrasive touches, the tone in which she reminded me about this. "I don't want to risk getting spotted by someone from one of the schools."

Setting off on my own, I found Manger Square and sat at a table in front of one of the cafes eating something called a "cordon bleu burger." As I was walking around afterward, a teenage boy called out to me, "*Shalom!*" laughing with some friends. What was that, an anti-Israeli dig? I didn't think Israelis were allowed to come here, though maybe any foreigner could serve as a proxy. I hated teenage boys in packs. They'd taunted me when I myself was a teenager, and here they were, still hassling me in middle age.

Greta was up at six-thirty the next morning. She made a fair amount of noise as she passed through the living room, where I slept on the couch.

I never wear sunglasses, but walking along Star Street, I had a rare desire for them. It was a day of overall glare, intensified by the almost white trough created by the stone-paved street and stone-faced buildings. The air was stuffy, full of something that bothered my sinuses, dust or pollutants. I reached the streets near the souk, where old women with heads covered by white scarves sat on the sidewalk with vegetables to sell; cauliflowers, piles of some kind of green leaf. A piece of Cologne Cathedral was on display, with a plaque saying an earlier piece had been destroyed in a "vicious incursion" by Israeli forces.

Back to Manger Square and another cordon bleu burger, with me sitting at the same table. Among all the changes and novelties of travel, I sometimes craved pure repetition. On steps leading down to the square sat five women holding framed pictures. They had their backs to me, preventing me from seeing the pictures, but I assumed these were of relatives killed by the Israelis. A local man took photographs of the women. Later, he brought chairs, and the old women, joined by a few old men, sat in a circle. Leaving the cafe, I saw the pictures they held were all of men.

Crossing the square, I ran into an English guy I'd met at the hotel in Amman. He was living in Bethlehem now, doing volunteer work. At the moment, he was handing out pamphlets for the Palestinian Prisoners' Society. He explained the photographs the women held were of prisoners, not people killed. The women met here every Thursday, not so much to make a statement to the foreign tourists who frequented the square, as I'd thought, more to have contact with each other, and be filmed and photographed by the Palestinian media.

In a reverse of my expectations, I'd found Ramallah livelier, more welcoming, and more connected to the outside world, while Bethlehem struck me as West Bank *profond*, backward and sullen, despite being closer to Jerusalem and more on the tourist route. If there was a theater here giving modern dance performances and a cafe like La Vie, I wasn't finding them.

After some unrewarding exploration, I walked up to the ridge and sat in the grounds of the University, reading. As I came down a street, I met the eyes of a man emerging from a house. "Where are you from?" he asked. The man told me he owned the hair salon in front of the house, a converted garage. He invited me inside. He'd decorated the interior himself, painting it in the colors of the Palestinian flag, red, black, and green. Small round images of Mozart were worked into the design like medallions, creating an odd blend of the West and the Middle East.

Montrelle told me he wasn't Muslim or even Arab. His relatives had come to this area with the Crusades, from some part of Europe. I'm not sure he specified which part, assuming he had accurate information on this point. Montrelle didn't look Arab; Italian perhaps.

Finding I was staying with a Couchsurfing host, he said he used to have a Couchsurfing profile, too. "I deleted it by accident, along with the five references I had. I want to create a new profile. Do you think maybe you could write me a reference for it?"

Smiling, puzzled, I said, "I'm not sure what sort of reference I could write. That we talked for a few minutes?"

I wondered what Montrelle's purpose was in accosting me. After a brief suspicion of sexual interest, his manner made this seem unlikely. A moment later, he offered to cut my hair for twenty-five shekels. "In the U.S., wouldn't it cost more like twenty dollars?" As a selling point, he said it would only take ten minutes. I questioned privately how good a ten minute haircut would be. Still, I had thin limp hair that soon returned to the same mediocre condition no matter whether I had a good cut or a bad one, and it was in need of some tidying. I let Montrelle go ahead.

As Montrelle snipped away, he told me he was looking after his eighty-year-old mother, who lived in the house. This kept him in Bethlehem, which he didn't like. The people here were too "complicated," he said. "Everyone knows everyone else's business."

Continuing down the road after my cut, I saw an Arab man enter the yard of the house through a side gate. He looked back at me, then looked again as he mounted some stairs, possibly cruising. Did he live with Montrelle? Was this a house of homosexual ill repute?

Greta returned late in the evening. She made herself dinner without offering me any and sat beside me on the couch eating it. Food is one of the trickiest aspects of surfing. I didn't expect Greta to provide room and board, and I wasn't especially hungry, yet it did feel odd to have to watch her eat.

I found myself biting my lip or running my tongue over my teeth, just to have something to do with my mouth.

Greta told more stories, one about a German friend who had married a Palestinian man. "Daysam went off to work in Germany, leaving Trudi here with their five children. A couple of years ago, she learned he'd married another woman in Germany – it's the custom in this culture to have more than one wife. Daysam was clever. He'd placed the children on his own passport, so if Trudi left the country, she couldn't take them with her and she'd lose custody. She's become a prisoner here."

I asked Greta if she'd dated Palestinian men. No, she said. "There are only a few men my age here who aren't already married. In any case, a Muslim wouldn't marry a non-Muslim, so if I got involved with someone, it would be clear to me and him and everyone else that marriage wasn't the goal. This is a small town. I don't want to get a reputation."

Greta noticed I'd gotten my hair cut. She was familiar with Montrelle, though she knew him by a different name, Donato. She said people had posted warnings on Couchsurfing about his preying on young male surfers. This suggested it might have been the Couchsurfing authorities who deleted his profile. One young surfer had contacted Greta late at night pleading to let him stay with her so he could escape from Montrelle-Donato's clutches. I refused to apologize for him as if our both being gay made us family members, saying only, "I'm insulted he didn't make a pass at me."

I revised my view of Greta from "abrasive" to "awkward." When I made her a present of some candy, she asked, "Why are you doing this?", though a simple "thank you" would have been more appropriate. She was someone who tended to say the wrong things in the wrong tone.

Greta made even more noise the following morning, sitting in the same room with me to use her laptop, crunching on cereal. Did she really imagine I could sleep through all that? Finally I just got up, in time to say goodbye to her.

The taxi driver who took me to the checkpoint tried to persuade me to visit his village on the way. He said, "It has the world's oldest olive tree." Tempting as this was, I declined.

The checkpoint wasn't what I expected. Not at all crowded, with only me and a handful of other travelers crossing over. Badly organized, so that while passing through three stages of security, showing my passport to bored young soldiers each time, I wasn't always sure where to go. Signs read Exit and Entrance, but exit and entrance to what? I didn't want to find myself back in the West Bank.

Soon I was at Jaffa Gate. Once again, I walked all the way to the Not Central Bus Station, though this did allow stops for lunch at a Thai restaurant and a used bookstore. The weather sultry today, making me cranky. At the station, my irritation showed when I stopped a woman from slipping in front of me in line to get through security, saying, "I'm ahead of you." A moment later, I wished I hadn't done this, for getting through with my cumbersome luggage took an especially long time, holding up the people behind me. My stir-fry and the long walk in the muggy weather made me pant with thirst, and I guzzled a Fanta as the bus rode along. The generic modern high-rises of Tel Aviv visible across the plain did at least give me a sense we were heading for a definite goal.

RONEN

I'd sent a Couchsurfing request to Ronen, my next host, because he was in the Gay Israel group. I was surprised to find he was attractive; this hadn't come across in the photographs in his profile. Shaved head, heavily lidded bedroom eyes, a trim body under a white T-shirt. He was witty, sharp; his apartment, small and messy. I was surprised to learn he earned extra money by cleaning people's homes, since his own didn't give any signs of skill in this area.

In his profile, Ronen said he had a dog. People had praised the dog in their references, saying she was sweet. When he responded to my request, Ronen mentioned a second dog, recently acquired. The female, Bess/Elizabeth, was indeed sweet. The male, Eddie/Edward (I suppose a third dog would have been named Jimmy/James or Annie/Anne to continue the theme of British royalty), was a fireball in himself, and also kept Bess, who might otherwise have been more calm, in a state of almost constant excitement. They barked at the drop of a hat, at passing dogs, at sounds outside I couldn't even identify; played together on the couch, nipping each other. "Don't put your bag on that chair," Ronen warned. "The dogs get up there." I thought, The dogs clearly go everywhere in this apartment they possibly can, without restriction.

Ronen fixed lunch for us, pasta with chicken. "I'll see to it you don't starve here," he said. "You know how Jewish people are, always offering you food."

"That's why I came to Israel," I said, "so Jewish mothers would offer me food."

Ronen made a face. "You just called me a Jewish mother."

"Jewish mothers and other Jewish people," I amended.

The worst dog moment was when Eddie barked at me, standing on the couch. I stood in front of him, hoping he would calm down if given a moment. Ronen was on his mobile with the telephone company, trying to get his internet connection fixed. He barked at me, too. "Walk away from him, walk away from him! Are you crazy?" Then he was mad because the person on the other end of the line, instead of holding on as he'd told her to, hung up. "She was just about to give me a break on my bill!" he snapped.

Ronen's bearish friend Gad came over. We walked the dogs, along with Gad's dog, plus a big old Labrador Gad was looking after for a friend. Ronen and Gad had met while hanging out with their dogs in a nearby park. I was in Dog World.

Ronen went off to a cleaning job. I used the unsecured internet of some neighbor, which flickered in and out. Frustrating, since I needed to communicate with the hosts I'd been lining up in Paris.

I'd accepted Gad's invitation to join him for more dog walking in the afternoon. First we walked all the dogs. Then, for Dog World reasons unclear to me, Gad returned Bess and Eddie to the apartment while we took the others to Yarkon Park. Gad slow of speech, but at least low-key and benign, as Ronen wasn't. Sexual fantasies about Ronen drifted in and out of my mind. I was half convinced he would suggest I join him in his bed that night rather than sleep on the couch in the living room. He'd mentioned that another male guest had planned to spend only a few days with him, then ended up staying much longer. Surely they must have slept together, I thought. There seemed more reasons to decline the invitation. That it would be awkward if sex didn't work out, yet I remained as a guest. That I wasn't sure I *liked* Ronen.

As I approached Ronen's front door, the dogs were at the bedroom window, barking furiously. They continued to bark after I entered. When Eddie at last stopped barking, he growled instead, which felt even more threatening, glaring at me with keen suspicion. I took care to make measured movements and not to turn my back on him. I could see tomorrow's headline, "Killer Cur KO's Couchsurfer."

Ronen returned at nine. Rather than thank me for washing the dishes he'd left in the sink, he asked where I'd put the ones on the drying rack. In the cupboard, I said. Acidly, "I'm not sure I appreciate guests rearranging my things." I didn't point out that I couldn't have put more dishes on the rack without stowing the ones already there.

I'd had warnings about Ronen earlier. At this point, a brilliantly illuminated sign appeared above the roadway exclaiming AGGRESSION. In my twenties, all I would have grasped was that Ronen was someone I wanted to have sex with. I would have been slow to figure out why our relationship went badly, why he was so unpleasant to me. Thankfully I was older now and a little wiser.

The outward manifestation of my taking this in was silence. Ronen noticed my withdrawal. It wasn't that the aggressive types weren't acute. "Are you okay?" he asked. "Are you just tired?"

Ronen and Gad walked the dogs. I had a feeling Ronen wasn't pleased that I didn't join them this time. My next host, David, had asked when I planned to arrive at his home on Saturday. I took the opportunity of Ronen's absence to call David and ask if I could come to his place a day early. He said he would look at his schedule and let me know tomorrow. That night, there was no invitation to join Ronen in his bedroom. Instead, he helped me make up the couch.

The next day, the dogs didn't bark at me, though I was alone in the apartment. While they might have started to accept me into the pack, I still found them unnerving, the way they watched my every move. What would qualify as a wrong one in their canine eyes?

Ronen had asked me to walk the dogs at around eleven. I managed to get Bess into her harness; she couldn't wear a collar, Ronen said, because Eddie might grab it in play and choke her. When I approached Eddie with his collar, he backed away, growling. Ronen's remark about the dishes had been the last straw that made me decide to depart early if possible; that Eddie wouldn't even let me put his collar on him was an extra straw. I called Gad, who came over and put the collar on Eddie, then left me to walk the dogs by myself.

After returning them to the apartment, I went to a mini-mall on Arlozorov Street. I found the mall tacky overall, though the cafe occupying part of the atrium was sleek and pleasant. I ordered hot water with mint. As I added sugar and stirred, making the mint leaves swirl around, I had a sudden realization. I saw I had the power to end my relationship with Ronen, such as it was; not to let it drag on, as I'd let other bad relationships in the past. The realization that almost brought tears to my eyes was that I could accomplish this goal even with a sort of *joy*, or at least good humor.

Combined with this, a sense of what a delight it was to be alive, to look at the other people sitting in the cafe, to listen to the agreeable music (a Karen Carpenter song at the moment), to sip my mint tea. I had trouble going as far as to love the ugly balloons filling the shaft of the atrium, but no matter.

David called later and told me I could come to his place that evening. When Ronen returned, I said I'd been talking with David, and he'd said if I liked I could come to his place earlier than scheduled. I was sure Ronen took in that I'd already packed my suitcase. Our conversation quite short – this was another delight, to realize that when I had to reject someone this way, he might have no more interest in prolonging the discussion than I did. I said only that I was having a problem with the dogs, not with him. Even within that context, I took the blame on myself, saying I'd overestimated the extent to which I was a "dog person."

I said, "I had a dog when I was a kid, but she was a sweet quiet Labrador."

Ronen gave a sour smile. "I know Labradors. Yours probably just wanted to lie there like a rug." Later, I realized his characterization had a critical edge: *his* dogs weren't like rugs, they were full of pep.

I mentioned to Ronen the business of Eddie not letting me put on his collar. He said, "You don't have to work for your keep, you know. Gad and I can walk the dogs." A movement toward accommodation on his part, but by this time my trajectory out of Dog World was already set.

DAVID

David was tall and thin, so thin I almost felt I was looking at him in a distorting fun-house mirror. His apartment was attractive, with a balcony surrounded by tree branches. The branches were still bare, spring having scarcely started, as I had to remind myself, despite the warmth of the days here. David had a middle-aged cat, Meowsi. After my time with Bess and Eddie, I wanted to scoop up small, sweet, soft-furred Meowsi and give her a big hug.

I took David out to dinner at a sushi restaurant on Bograshov, where we sat outside. David was another American-Israeli cross, with his family moving back and forth between the two countries while he grew up. His English sounded American. He pronounced some words with unusual precision, like "autumn," equally accenting both syllables, though I was unclear what this told me about his background.

"Lots of Israelis want to emigrate to the U.S.," David said.

"Not to Europe?" I asked.

"No," he said. "The U.S. is usually the goal."

Some people made *aliyah*, I reflected, "the ascent to Israel," while others made a contrasting movement. The descent from Israel, I supposed.

David worked for an NGO managing water usage in the region. The organization had offices in Israel, the West Bank, and Jordan, each staffed by locals. It tried to convince people that water issues must be addressed by all three countries working together. Israel's main aquifer was under the West Bank. Because the water ran downhill, if Israel took too much water from its wells, the Palestinian wells would go dry. On the other hand, if Palestinians polluted the water under their land, that would affect Israel.

"Some Israelis question my loyalty because I'm working with the other two groups," David said. "Taking a job with the organization is even more of a black mark against the Palestinians and Jordanians. It can make it hard for them to find other work in their countries. They're seen as traitors colluding with the enemy."

David had both surfed and hosted, and talked about some of his experiences. He said he wanted to hear about "the guy with the dogs," and I told him the story, with the Greta tale as an adjunct. "With Greta," I said, "I had a lesson in holding off a bit before I abandoned ship. With Ronen, a lesson in when to abandon it."

The next day was a Saturday, Shabbat again. Up until now, Tel Aviv had seemed far removed from the religiosity of Jerusalem. In the sunny weather, it could pass for a town in Southern California, with lots of people heading for the beach, young guys in trunks, people carrying surfboards. Today, the empty streets and closed shops reminded me I was definitely in Israel.

Although the restaurants had opened again by the evening, David suggested we make dinner ourselves. He worked on potato pancakes while I made a green salad and a veggie stir fry. If I were designing an ideal Couchsurfing guest, I would include a flare for cooking. A salad and a stir fry were about the extent of my own skills.

David had spent much of the day at a meeting of an Israeli-Palestinian group he belonged to discussing the peace process. The group alternated between meeting in Ramallah and Jerusalem, with either one contingent or the other having to get special passes. The three Palestinians and three Israelis communicated through a translator.

They'd gotten stuck on the very first point in the Israeli paper, which linked the Jewish refugees from the 1948 war with Palestinian ones. "The Palestinians refused to accept the comparison," David told me while we ate. "They argued there were no Jewish refugees. I said the father of my first Israeli girlfriend had had to flee Alexandria because of the war, and the family of my second girlfriend to run away from Morocco. They didn't want to hear any of this. The Palestinians are so – " He made a gesture of narrow focus, placing his hands a few inches apart in front of his eyes. "They want to see their tragedy as the only one in the world, the greatest."

After a half hour spent on this single point, they'd moved on to others, and on these the two contingents were more in accord. "The Israelis agreed to full right of return for the Palestinians. We wanted the same right for Jewish refugees, while knowing most of these wouldn't actually use it. Would my ex-girlfriend's father want to leave his comfortable home in Israel and return to his house in Alexandria? Probably not."

David said, "In the eyes of the U.N., the Palestinian refugees are the only ones in the world who pass on their rights to their children. That means something like five million Palestinians could ask to return to their homes in Israel. What if one couple had six children, and these six children each had six more? How would the ancestral home be divided? What if it had been torn down and replaced with a high-rise? Should the high-rise be replaced with a re-creation of the original stone house? The Palestinians were completely blithe about all these considerations. Arab families had ways of arranging these things, they said. One family member might want to live in the house, another not."

Impatient with the Palestinians, I said, "Why don't the Israelis just pay them off?"

"That's what most of us want to do," David responded. "We'd find the money somewhere. Germany did that after the war with Holocaust victims. There were huge protests about it here in Israel. People called it blood money. Still, all the reparation money was crucial for Israel at the time, when it was very poor."

When I asked David how he felt about the future of the country, he said with a smile, "Oh, Israel will be destroyed someday, if things continue as they are. There will be one war we won't win, after so many we have. It will all be over before any other country has time to react. Israel is such a small place, it would be easy to bomb it into a wasteland in a very short time. If we try to flee, where can we go? We're surrounded by hostile neighbors."

"What's keeping you here in that case?" I said. "You've got U.S. citizenship. You could easily emigrate."

David shrugged. "I'm willing to take my chances in Israel. Sometimes I'm not exactly sure why."

Arriving at Ben-Gurion Airport a couple of days later, I was stuck in a long, slow line at the security check. Baseem had told me and the French couple horror stories about harassment and interrogations at the airport, enjoying any chance to portray the Israelis in a bad light. One story was about a girl from Santa Barbara whose laptop the security people confiscated, then sent to her home with a bullet through the screen.

When I'd expressed concern about getting questioned at the airport myself, Baseem had said, "You don't need to worry. You don't look like an activist."

I made a joke out of this, pouting.

"No, you look like a potato," Baseem said, maybe thinking of "couch potato."

More comic pouting from me: "I'm not a potato!"

Odette kindly suggested, "You're a sweet potato."

This was the first airport I'd encountered where your luggage was scanned before you checked it in. Guards questioned people. My interview didn't start well.

"When did you enter Israel?" the guard snapped.

"I think on March ninth. You can check the date in my passport – "

"I don't want to check your passport, I want you to tell me."

"I think it was on March ninth."

"Were you here for business or tourism?"

"Tourism." The guard asked where I'd gone in the country. Preferring to err on the side of caution, I didn't tell him I'd visited the West Bank. I'd removed all evidence of the trip, telephone numbers from my mobile, some photographs from my camera.

The guard waved me on. Whether Couchsurfer, couch potato, or sweet potato, I made it onto the plane without further incident.

Sometimes I loved plane flights, at least ones that weren't too long; loved the enforced idleness, the permission to let my mind wander. I thought again of appearing in my high school's production of *Fiddler on the Roof*. My journal told the story of opening night. "I went on and *was* Mendel. Hands on hips, filling out my clothes, gesturing. Strong, like Mr. Richards wanted. I walked like a man on stage, squeezed into the high black boots, my pants tucked in the tops, the fringe of my shawl jiggling. I encountered someone else, not Mendel really, but not really me either. Perhaps a dark, handsome, striding man who was potential in me."

The theater was a life-saver for me, as for many other shy, awkward teenagers, my drama class like a daily group therapy session. And it was my appearance in *Fiddler* that gave me the biggest glimpse of another person who was, as I said, potential in me, a self-confident adult male.

In its day, *Fiddler* was a ground-breaking musical in terms of its subject matter. Still, it understandably gave the audience "pogrom lite" at the end of the story. At least in my high school's production, the attacking Russians didn't kill anyone or as much as break a window. When the constable told us we must pack our things and abandon our village in three days, he made clear he was only following orders. Dressed in our strangely new-looking and spotless peasant costumes, we shetel dwellers gathered on stage for "Anatevka," the final number. We admitted that Anatevka wasn't much, this scrappy, scruffy middle-of-nowhere place. Still, it was our home, where we'd lived all our lives and knew everyone we passed in the street. Yente the matchmaker was played by Samantha Clark, a sturdy handsome blonde who was always chewing gum off-stage. Lacking a solo, she apparently decided to make "Anatevka" her big moment. Wearing a white wig and crudely aged by a fellow thespian's makeup job, she used her powerful voice to crest over the rest of the cast, stretching out her hands in hammy lamentation.

I doubted any of us grasped much more about this song than that it was sad. Yet, along with other influences, something must have registered with me and maybe the other kids. Why else, when I went away to college and reveled in access to a library that was much bigger and more sophisticated than the public one in my home town, did I seek out the shelves with Holocaust narratives?

I didn't remember "Anatevka" ever making me cry when we sang it in my high school production. Forty years later, during this visit to Israel and the West Bank, every time it started up in my mind, the tears came. I saw Samantha Clark and the rest of us traipsing along a road in a bleak landscape, our belongings heaped into pitiful little carts. Sometimes in my imagination we were shtetel dwellers, sometimes we were other sorts of refugees, Jews desperately rushing into Israel, Palestinians desperately pouring out.

Chapter 4

Paris: The Boy Friend

At the RER station in de Gaulle airport, the woman at the ticket window started our talk with "Bonjour." Her tone implied, "Since this may be the first time you speak to a French person on your visit, I need to train you to begin every conversation with 'Bonjour.'" Cooperating like a good pupil, I responded, "Bonjour," then switched to English, not yet ready to unsheathe my bad French.

France wasn't one country, but two. There was Fantasy France whipped up by books and films, which most people encountered, and Real France, which a smaller number of people had a chance to experience. *The Boy Friend*, a cheery musical set in the Riviera and staged at my college during my freshman year, embodied for me Fantasy France, the France of berets, baguettes, and *sacrebleu!* This France posed few language difficulties beyond, "*Oui, Madame*" and "*N'est-ce pas?*" Most of the main characters weren't French in any case, rather vacationing English. *Fiddler* was forward-looking in its day; *The Boy Friend*, a Fifties revisiting of Twenties musicals, looked resolutely backward. It was a distillation of a distillation, doubly removed from any roots in reality. As often happened, this musical more perfectly embodied what we considered the spirit of the period than anything made at the time, and had a strange unadventurous charm.

I tried out for the chorus and was accepted. Probably everyone who tried out was accepted, considering how small my school was. As one of the few men with even a smidgen of dance experience, thanks to my taking ballet for half a year in high school, the director corralled me into partnering one of the women chorus members in the Act III tango.

There's nothing like taking part in a musical to etch it indelibly into your brain. The sweet naivete of this show, strung out along a staggeringly basic boy-meets-girl story line, meshes with the naivete of my freshman year. I can still remember most of the lyrics the chorus sings, and any mention of Nice is sure to kick off in my mind the song "It's Nicer in Nice."

College also provided my first encounter with Real France, aside from a week in Paris at sixteen as part of a student tour through Europe, too short a time for much reality to sink in. In my junior year at UC Santa Cruz, I applied to study abroad. I asked to go to the U.K. There was a lot of competition for that placement, and instead I was assigned to France because I'd studied French. On the advice of returning students, I ranked Bordeaux last in preference out of a half-dozen universities. Alas, that was where my school sent me, since Bordeaux had the largest number of slots.

I won't nitpick at the way the French dealt with me as a complete stranger during my year as an exchange student. Instead, I'll only give the example of someone who did have an acquaintance with me, my landlady, Madame Pince. After she collected me from the train station in a taxi and deposited me in my room on the top floor of the apartment building where she lived, I had almost no contact with her. When my heater broke and I went downstairs to her apartment, she had me wait in the hall while she fetched another one. Wouldn't an Italian or a Spaniard have invited me in for a few minutes of chat, the poor clueless young American alone in a foreign country?

Dealings with the French later in life perpetuated my mixed feelings. Several years before my Couchsurfing travels, as my ex and I got on a long-distance bus after crossing into France from Spain, the driver scolded me for trying to bring a banana on board and made me stow it in my suitcase in the hold. I couldn't imagine a bus driver in Spain, the land of Do Whatever You Want Within Reasonable Limits, forbidding on-board bananas.

I go on an alert in France. Not a red or even an orange alert; maybe a pale yellow one. I'm always slightly braced for some slightly unpleasant encounter. Wherever I travel, I avoid asking people for directions unless I'm truly at a loss, and I go to even greater avoidant lengths in France. A couple of times on a trip to Paris in my forties, I'd had no choice. Neither of the resulting encounters was exactly heart-warming. In the second, the woman I asked, in French, how to get to Boulevard du Montparnasse looked at me with an expression that said, "Your asking me that question is by far the worst thing that could have happened to me today."

An interaction on the same trip offered me a clue to the French attitude toward strangers. I was sitting on a bench in the park at Versailles, beside that long, long, long artery leading to the Grand Canal that's splendid to cast your eyes down from the palace, but tedious to get your body down on foot. A middle-aged Frenchwoman approached. She was so sorry to disturb me – "desolated to disarrange me," to translate literally – but could she ask me a question? Of course, I said. She asked if I knew how to get to the Bosquet de l'Étoile. People from other countries might not have bothered with more of a preliminary than "Excuse me" or dispensed with one altogether. This woman believed she must placate the outrage I was sure to feel at being intruded on by a stranger. Unfortunately, looking at my map, I had to tell her that the Bosquet de l'Étoile lay on the other side of the long, long, long carpet of grass in the middle of the long, long, long artery. This was a *pelouse interdite*, a prohibited lawn that she wasn't allowed to walk on.

By the point in my life when I made my Couchsurfing voyage, I had if not exactly a love-hate relationship with France, maybe a like-dislike one. However, the like was strong enough for me to want to return.

ROLAND

Buying a ticket from the "Bonjour" lady, I took the RER into central Paris, then the metro to Place de la République to meet my first host, Roland. Although I thought I'd been gaining confidence with my Couchsurfing, I did have a moment of trepidation as I stood before the imposing stone facade of Roland's apartment building, its entrance large enough for five gendarmes to enter abreast with five more standing on their shoulders. True, Roland wasn't my first host, but he was the first of the French persuasion.

Roland was forty, with a big strong nose, sketchy goatee, and beautiful curly brown hair, a couple of locks of which spiraled down his forehead. His apartment had a large salon with a narrow balcony running along one side and looked like it might have appeared in a French edition of *Architectural Digest*.

It was furnished with Deco pieces Roland had brought back from Chile, where he'd spent the first eight years of his work life. "Most of them were made in Europe," he said, smiling, "so I was only returning them to their place of origin." Interesting and diverse art on the walls, most of which had also come from Chile. Not at all the sort of apartment I would expect to Couchsurf in. Roland offered me a drink along with hors d'oeuvres of olives, sausage slices, and pistachios. I took a deep breath and started to relax.

I offered to take Roland out to dinner. Crossing Boulevard du Temple, he said this was the border between the third and eleventh arrondissements. "Property on the other side of the street is worth twenty percent more just because it's in the third." We wandered around the Haut Marais; wandered a particularly long time, since the owner of the crêperie we decided on told us to return in forty minutes, the place was so crowded. In fact, all the cafes we passed were crowded. Roland told me that Tuesday, Wednesday, and Thursday were the nights when Parisians went out to eat, before people flooded in from outside Paris on the weekend. I nodded, thinking, "Doesn't that mean the restaurants are almost always crowded, just with different people?" He said many of the residents in this neighborhood were "bobos," bourgeois bohemians.

Finally dinner, *crêpes salées* followed by a *crêpe sucrée* that we split. To drink, hard cider. To my left, a white man and woman with a black man. On the other side, a German woman and her little boy, who read a book during part of the meal. I liked both sets of neighbors. Strange how we could be happy, or not, with people sitting near us in a public place, without ever interacting with them. Although in this case, our tables were so close to each other that nearness almost amounted to interaction.

Roland was easy to talk with, smiling often. Where were the tense French I remembered from earlier visits? He did have a habit of finishing a verbal paragraph, then, when I started to speak, interrupting me and starting another paragraph of his own. Roland worked for an organization that helped French companies extend their business to foreign countries, a sort of non-governmental chamber of commerce. Since it only had seven employees, Roland had to perform many different tasks. He liked this, though it kept him very busy.

"France is in decline," Roland said. "Soon, it will just be a museum full of pretty things." I asked, if Germany could continue to have a strong economy, why couldn't France? The answer, according to Roland, was that French companies were smaller and tended be family-run and conservative, not interested in innovation.

Encouraged by my cider, I said a few things in French. Roland was surprised I spoke French. Most Americans didn't. Still, I knew I was making mistakes right and left. He pointed out that I said, "*Je suis heureuse*," which translated as, "I'm a happy girl."

I slept in Roland's office, which was dark and quiet. I used a fold-out couch, a *clic-clac*. So called because a click signaled that a mechanism had engaged or disengaged, allowing you to flatten out the couch or fold it up. Unfortunately, the *clic-clac* had a hard seam running across the middle right where I lay. Since Roland didn't have a key for me, in the morning I needed to get up in time to leave with him at eight-thirty. If he didn't want me in his posh apartment while he wasn't there, I couldn't blame him.

Roland appeared looking *très chic*, as I told him, in a beautiful suit. His apartment was stuffed with clothes and accessories like hats and shoulder bags. I counted twenty ties on one tie rack in the study. He wore a shirt to work only once, he said, then had it cleaned.

"I like to eat a real breakfast," Roland told me, standing in the kitchen. All he meant by this was that he ate a little fruit, a slice of bread, and a tiny container of yogurt, rather than virtually nothing like most French people.

Since I needed to be out all day, I went to the Louvre. To my surprise and displeasure, I found the museum allowed photography. A man actually tapped my shoulder and asked me to move so he could snap a photo of a Titian. I almost gave a French cry of exasperation.

When I returned that evening, Roland was back in the kitchen. He said, "I don't want you to think I always do this . . ." I worried he was going to say, "I don't always feed my Couchsurfing guests, but since you haven't offered to take me out again, I suppose I'll have to." Then he finished his thought, that he didn't always have a drink at the end of the day. Roland did make dinner, heating up a chicken casserole he'd prepared a couple of days before.

"Do you want your salad first?" he asked.

"No," I said, "I'll just have everything on one plate at the same time. We Americans are uncivilized. We don't believe in courses."

Roland had already mentioned having a girlfriend. I thought we knew each other well enough by now for me to ask some questions about her. Roland said, "When I was younger, I planned to marry and have children. At this point, it looks like at least the children part won't happen." This girlfriend was older than he was and almost beyond the age of having children, unlike his previous girlfriend, who had been twenty-seven. Roland held Paris partly responsible for his single state. "There are too many distractions here, too much to do.

Paris is like New York, a city of single people. Half the population is unmarried."

Roland had told me yesterday he would look for a spare key to his apartment at his office. Now he said he couldn't find it. With another long day ahead of me, I went to the Centre Pompidou. A guard approached me while I was making notes about a painting and told me I couldn't use a pen. In an encounter with a French person in France, I became very French myself. "*On ne peut pas écrire ici?*" I questioned irritably: you can't write here? "*Avec un crayon, oui,*" he said: with a pencil, which of course I didn't have. The fear that someone might scribble on a painting wasn't completely unreasonable, yet why was it only the French who acted on it this way? I'd never known any other museum where a guard would stop you from writing with a pen.

Parting from Roland the following morning, in an outgoing moment, I suggested we get together again later in my visit. "Well, perhaps we could meet for coffee," he said. He sounded hesitant, and for a moment I couldn't help feeling my old bugbear had returned. The French being reserved, the French keeping me at arm's length.

OLIVIER

My next host lived on a dead-end street near Place de Clichy. Olivier was about my age, tall, *bronzé*, well-built. His years showed in his neck, that vulnerable point in both combat and aging. He led the way in exchanging air kisses, whereas Roland had shaken my hand. Must be a gay guys together thing, I thought. Olivier's green eyes swept downward, taking in my appearance. I was about to say I caught him at this, while in truth he might not have made any attempt at concealment.

I started by speaking French with him. However, his better English soon prevailed.

Olivier's apartment was attractive in a different way from Roland's. In this case, the beauty was created almost entirely by means of books. Other than bookshelves, the living room contained practically no furniture except a small couch at one end. An amazing book collection, reminding me of some French version of the old house in *Fahrenheit 451* with its huge private library that goes up in flames. Novels, books on art, photography. "Once I thought about repainting the apartment," Olivier said. "By the time I cleared the shelves on one side, I realized my books made this just too big a job."

Olivier gave me keys. When I mentioned that Roland hadn't, Olivier said most French hosts wouldn't. "As for me, I don't worry about people taking things. I hardly have anything worth stealing."

Olivier had a steady gaze, tranquil and tranquilizing. I wondered if there was any sexual spark between us. At one point while we talked, when his eyes were half closed, I realized he had large eyelids. That was part of the beauty of his eyes.

I offered to take Olivier out for lunch. Instead, he said he would make it. He prepared the sort of meal I would, a big salad that included rice and vegetables. Olivier managed a dance studio in the Marais. He carried himself well, and I assumed he'd been a dancer himself. It turned out he hadn't. Instead, he'd returned to school in his thirties to get a degree in managing arts organizations and just happened to fall into a job in the dance world. Olivier talked about how many cultural things there were to do in Paris, though he was less enthusiastic about the gay scene. "At my age, I've become invisible," he said and imitated someone looking away with an elaborate show of disinterest.

"I think that's true in gay culture everywhere," I said, "from Paris to Timbuktu."

After lunch, Olivier set off to visit relatives in Normandy, saying he would return at seven tomorrow evening. I'd heard of this from other Couchsurfers, a host letting a guest stay in his home while he wasn't there. In some cases, the host and guest never even met, a mutual friend possibly handing over the keys.

Although I'd offered to take Olivier out to dinner tomorrow, he'd suggested I just make something myself. I was comfortable doing this since I could follow in his footsteps with a dinner salad that wouldn't overtax my cooking skills. I assumed Olivier would want to eat as soon as he got home – but no, this was France, so he postponed eating until eight.

While we waited for dinner time, we sat on the couch, necessarily close since it was so small. Olivier told me about the love of his life, an Italian he'd met in the Paris metro in the mid Eighties (exchange of looks on the platform, rubbing knees on the train). Nari had been a teacher, and making careful use of their vacation time, they'd managed to spend a third of the year together.

"When the test for HIV came out," Olivier said, "Nari tested positive. I was sure I would, too. In fact, I assumed I must have infected him. I'd had sex with lots of guys, whereas Nari lived in a small town near Milan, he wasn't out to his family, and he'd only had sex with maybe six men in his whole life. Instead, when I was tested, I found I was negative. It was just one of those bizarre things." He told me that Nari had died a couple of years later.

After Nari, Olivier told me, he hadn't wanted another boyfriend. He'd only just been entering his thirties at that point, and privately I wondered if this was too soon to retire from the world of boyfriendship. Perhaps one of the many human stratagems for limiting involvement had been at work, that of "I've already had the love of my life and don't need another." Olivier told me that nowadays he had a circle of men he had sex with. He also exchanged massages with other gay guys and some of his erotic energy was channeled into this. He talked about choosing the music for a session, comparing it to a dance performance; how he paid attention to the man's body, looking for signals. As we talked about getting an erection during a massage, and Olivier placed his hand on my leg in demonstration of some point, I was looking for signals, too. Was he interested, was I?

After dinner, Olivier asked if I wanted to watch a movie. He suggested a French version of *Lady Chatterley's Lover*, which he'd bought recently. Surely someone didn't suggest watching *Lady Chatterley's Lover* if he didn't want to send a signal. Especially when the television was in Olivier's bedroom, and to watch it, we had to sit on his bed, our backs against the wall. We didn't touch, nor did we speak much, except when I made a joke about understanding all the French in one of many sex scenes in which the leads didn't utter a word, only sighed and gave little cries. During the closing credits, I finally galvanized myself into making at least a move toward a move.

"If it weren't so late," I said, "I'd suggest we try acting out one of those scenes ourselves."

Olivier looked at me from beneath his large eyelids and said, "It is very late, isn't it?"

The French could be difficult to read, and so could gay men, and so could perhaps above all a French gay man.

TINO AND JAMES

Conveniently, the home of my next hosts, Tino and James, was close enough for me to reach on foot. Tino was from an Italian family, though raised in France. He was Italian in coloring, though slight and small, with the body almost of an adolescent. Tino was lively, and we had an instant rapport. James, his American partner, was much younger, stout. That seemed the trade-off, youth provided, but not slenderness, though maybe in truth Tino wasn't bothered by the stoutness. James had eyes that were enormous in a way that wasn't exactly attractive. They appeared hard, strange, with some element of the artificial about them, as if they'd been unnaturally enlarged in some culture.

James had just quit his job working for a gay news website, tired of getting paid so little and so late by his boss. Before that, he'd spent two years teaching English in France. He'd been put into classrooms with no training, his time divided inconveniently among several different schools. Overall, he made this sound like a fairly horrible experience, eliminating any impulse on my part to say, "If only I'd done that at his age." It also suggested why many French people didn't speak English well. Since Tino himself was typical in this respect, despite an American partner, I used my ramshackle French. Tino was an actor and playwright. This accounted for their both being home on a weekday, the one's lack of a job and the other's erratic schedule.

I heard how Tino and James had met in a sauna in Clermont-Ferrand, where Tino was visiting his family and James was teaching English in a high school at the time. They entered into a civil union, which in theory earned James a couple of one-year visas. "The Catch-22 was that to get the first visa, I had to prove I'd lived with Tino for twelve months by providing utility bills with my name on them. The authorities didn't explain how I was supposed to have lived legally in France for a year without a visa." James's solution was to continue teaching for another year, now in Paris, and renew his work visa.

The state owned the building where Tino and James lived. Tino had only been able to secure an apartment here because at the time he was working as a guard at the Louvre. "We'll have to stay here until we die," James said, "because there's no way we can find another place in Paris we can afford." The one-bedroom apartment was sparsely furnished and not especially clean. The toilet bowl looked as if it hadn't been scrubbed properly for such a long time that, at this point, no further effort would have any effect.

Tino talked about his work as a guard; how guards in the same room would tell each other their life's story to pass the time; how the job was so boring, some guards went insane. The guards were either artistic types like him or ex-military. Tino imitated a jaded guard directing an American tourist to the Mona Lisa, though as I pointed out, there were signs everywhere in the museum showing where it was. He told a story about picking up a Jesuit priest during his guard duties and later having sex with him in bushes near the museum, with the priest saying this was wrong, but going ahead anyway. Thrown in, the detail that the priest had a big cock. A standard feature of gay sex stories: ". . . and he had a big cock."

James had some funny stories of his own, one about a straight man who posed as a lesbian blogger in Iran, at one point claiming he'd been kidnapped by the Iranian government. "So remember," he said, "on the internet, don't be too sure you know who anyone really is." Still, it was clear to me from the outset that I liked Tino more. I thought of other couples I knew and considered whether a preference for one partner or another was almost inevitable.

After spending several years in France, James spoke fluent, though American-accented French. He was frustrated that Tino wouldn't practice his English with me. Privately I was pushing for French. If I couldn't think of a French word or phrase, I could always ask James. In some cases, we had trouble finding a French equivalent, for "carried away" and "misguided." The three of us had an interesting discussion as to whether there was a word in French that had the exact meaning of "friendly." James maintained there wasn't, "and what does that tell you about the French?" When Tino spoke English, he kept referring to men as "she."

"*Qu'est-ce que c'est 'salop'?*" I asked, puzzled by a word I'd found in a couple of French profiles on a dating website.

"It means 'slut,'" James explained.

"Ah gay life," I laughed, "where people *advertise* themselves as sluts!"

I took Tino and James out to dinner at a restaurant near the Opéra Garnier. As we sat down at our table and I anticipated dealing with a French waiter, my yellow alert light burned a little brighter. I was sure that a main source of the reputation the French had for rudeness was the classic French waiter. Ten years before when my ex and I went out to dinner with a French couple visiting San Francisco, the husband, Roger, was struck by the way our American waiter talked to us: offering advice about which dishes we should order, joking with us. In France, he said, waiters were trained to keep their distance from customers, maintaining *un visage neutre*, a neutral face.

"The waiter should appear neither happy nor sad," Roger explained. "He'll tell you what's in a dish, though not which one he thinks is best. If you ask him for a recommendation, he'll say that everything on the menu is good." Most French people would find our American waiter "too familiar."

Plausible enough. However, I'd had French waiters behave in ways Roger's gloss didn't cover. On a visit to Paris, my ex and I had dinner with our English friends Jane and Eileen. When the waiter brought two of us our first courses, I asked if we could have some bread. "*Évidemment*," he said, "I'll bring it after I've served madame her food," gesturing at Eileen. His "evidently" and his tone communicated that I shouldn't pester him.

Instead of an unsmiling waiter, Tino, James, and I were handed our menus by a smiling waitress. I commented on how like an American waitress she was. She even stopped by the table after we'd started eating to ask if everything was satisfactory.

James's parents had visited the week before. "Do they get along with Tino?" I asked.

James said, "They do, they like him. Their only concern is that he's too old for me."

"But you have a young spirit," I said to Tino, laying my hand on his arm.

Tino asked me some questions about my own family. James listened, without saying anything himself. This reinforced my sense of Tino as the more adult of the two. Taking an interest in others was a quality I found more often in older people.

To return to Porte de Clichy, we rented bikes from a Vélib stand. This was one of those moments when I was glad to be Couchsurfing. Only a few days after arriving in Paris, here I was skimming along on a bike with two locals; a bike I would have had difficulty obtaining on my own, lacking a European credit card. The statues bedecking the Opéra Garnier seemed to grow larger as we approached. When we paused at an intersection, Tino, in that attentive way he had, checked to see what speed I was using. Leaning over, he switched me to third, saying this was better for the slight uphill we were on.

As soon as we arrived home, the two men took off their shoes and – in an unexplained ritual – their pants. They got out their laptops, which they used half-reclining on their bed.

I slept on another *clic-clac*, this one more comfortable than Roland's.

Tino and James gave a dinner party the next evening, kindly including me. The first guest to arrive was Henri, whom Tino had met while working at the Louvre. Henri was in charge of the museum's keys. He told me how many there were, though with my usual obtuseness about numbers in foreign languages, I wasn't sure of the exact figure. Something astonishing, perhaps twelve hundred.

I already knew from Tino that after Henri had broken up with his partner seven years ago, not wanting an apartment of his own, he'd lived with various friends. "I can see someone doing that for seven months," I'd said, "but not seven *years*." Henri had lived with Tino for the longest time, leaving only when James moved in, since the apartment wasn't big enough for three. While he lived with Tino, Henri would buy food for the household, though he'd only paid rent when Tino was out of town for long periods performing. Tino had told me Henri lived very simply, with few possessions.

When Tino asked Henri how he was, Henri said he'd spent four hours at the dentist yesterday. He had two dentists, though I wasn't clear how the labor was divided between them. With him talking about dentists, I had to make an effort not to drop my eyes to his teeth. On a couple of occasions when I couldn't help myself, I saw that he had too many, with some crowding others into odd positions.

Next, a couple arrived, Gaston and Lorraine. Gaston worked as a guard at the Louvre at night. Because this was a less popular shift, it earned him three months of vacation a year. Lorraine was a guard during the day. "Are there ghosts in the Louvre?" I asked. "Yes," Gaston said, "especially near the old *donjon* below the Renaissance building. Ghosts of soldiers who died attacking its walls or while imprisoned inside. I haven't seen any of them myself, though other guards have."

I sat between Gaston and Lorraine. Gaston was the male magnetic pole I oriented myself toward. With his scraggly beard concealing a deficient chin and long hair in a pony tail, he wasn't someone I found instantly sexy. Still, he had the appeal of being twenty years younger than I was, and his conversation was witty, sparkling. He talked more than anyone else, out-talking even talkative Tino. The conversation was lively and smart, about movies, other topics. A fair amount of food talk, about wine, ice cream. Self-conscious about his teeth, Henri held his hand over his mouth when he laughed, like a Japanese woman. He was slightly disapproving of the story I told about locking myself in the toilets at the Louvre whenever I wanted a snack, retrieving crackers and cheese slices from my shoulder bag.

James said the least. After serving the first course, he made a sharp little complaint that Tino didn't sit down at once so people could start eating – so *he* could start, since he was plainly someone always eager, almost desperate, to eat.

At first my French was adequate, both for following what others said and saying things myself. As the evening went on and I felt the effects of a couple of glasses of wine, my French deteriorated and my mind as a whole, so that I couldn't remember the name of the German actor in *Jules et Jim*, among other things. The ceiling light was covered with a shade of woven fibers. The light it cast made it look like we were inside a huge bird's nest, one that rocked in the breeze from the open window.

After we'd drunk a bottle of Tino's white wine, he opened Gaston's red, which had come in a decorative box. He opened the bottle I'd brought only when that, too, was empty. I'd caught Tino making some disparaging remark about the wine I'd contributed to our lunch on the first day of my visit.

"At least this wine is better than what I brought before," I said to him hopefully.

"The wine you brought before was bad," Tino frowned. "This one is *moyen*," so-so. Maybe as the wine was making me more dim-witted, it was making Tino more blunt. James intervened, trying to silence Tino's complaints. Tino responded that he wasn't serious, though clearly he was to some extent. I tried to laugh off the matter by saying, "I'm an uncouth American, so naturally I don't know anything about wine." I hoped I'd never mentioned to them that I'd grown up in Napa Valley.

Tino and Gaston dispensed tips about how to determine if a wine was good. The bottle should have an indented bottom, it needed to have an R not an N on the seal, and to be bottled at the chateau or, better yet, the *domaine* (the distinction between the two unclear to me). Which years were good, though this could vary from one region to another. "Next time, I'll bring flowers," I said to Lorraine in an aside.

The following day, I walked through the Luxembourg Gardens. I recalled coming here on my last visit to Paris twelve years ago and noticing how individually dressed the French were, the women wearing scarves and preferring skirts to slacks, the men in discretely stylish clothes. Some of the choices odd, the colors and combinations of patterns, yet at least always interesting.

Today, I saw mostly French who looked more like Americans, or more accurately, like generic Westerners, casually and unadventurously dressed, possibly in clothes from the Gap nearby on Boulevard Saint-Michel. I remembered Catherine, Roger's wife, being astonished that in San Francisco so many people went about their everyday activities in *vêtements de sport*, sports clothes. Since then, it appeared many French people had adopted this lazy, boring approach to dress, where you wore the same clothes to walk in the Luxembourg Gardens as to work in your own garden. At least Roland was upholding the old standards in his work clothes.

I thought I detected another change. The French appeared to be turning out more smiles than before; smiles that, I'd had French people tell me in the past, they thought Americans dispensed too freely, so that they became meaningless. The French were more smiling and more relaxed. Had they changed, or was it more that my perceptions had, influenced by my staying not in a hotel or hostel, instead with several likable French hosts (I forgave Tino for criticizing my wine)? Or was it just that *I* was more relaxed among them on this visit, older and wiser? What did it matter if a waiter told me, "*Evidently* I'll bring the bread"? I could simply respond with the debased currency of one of my American smiles. My alert light dimmed to the palest possible yellow, almost flickered out. At the dinner party, when I'd questioned whether the French were changing, Gaston joked, "If they are, it's thanks to Prozac. France has one of the highest usages in the world."

Where were the French of yesteryear? All or mostly melted away? Would I never again have to deal with a crusty old-school French waiter? I felt this possible loss in a particular way. I'd always believed that the same qualities in the French that caused me problems were the ones that would make them understand me. The French could be irritable, critical, and so could I. I was sure that if I made a calculation, the words that appeared most often in my journal were "complain," as in "I complained," and "annoyed," as in "I was annoyed." Once after attending a meeting of a Spanish language group, I'd voiced to a Mexican friend my irritation at the way the leader had conducted it. My friend couldn't tune into irritation. In the end, I gave up and tuned instead into his cheerful acceptance. "Miguel takes the trouble to organize the group," my friend said, "so my attitude is he can lead it the way he wants." By nature, my temperament leaned toward the French. Through working on myself, I wanted to cultivate what I thought of as a more good-humored Mexican side.

According to Wikipedia, *The Boy Friend* is a "perennial favorite of amateur groups due to its relatively small cast and low production costs." My recollection is that the staging at my college, thrown together in a few weeks, had closer to no production costs. I'm not absolutely sure there was a set. We men in the chorus were left largely to our own devices for costumes, with the director asking us to wear white pants and black shoes, though we were at least given straw boaters. The accompaniment was provided by the director banging on an upright piano. Mid-winter, most of the cast got sick, no doubt by being youthfully careless about sharing glasses backstage. The boy and girl leads were good, however, and I always took care in the last act to listen from the sidelines as the girl sang "Poor Little Pierrette." By leading more than following, my dance partner Debbie got me through the tango without major mishaps.

"I can't believe I agreed to be in this," Mike Ligda, the preceptor of my dorm, said to me one day at rehearsals. "I've got a million other things I should be doing."

I shook my head in sympathy, equally amazed that I had agreed. I feel sure that if I tracked down Mike today and asked if he was glad he'd found time to appear in *The Boy Friend*, he'd say, "Absolutely!"

And now I was in Paris, in Real France, and the French seemed nicer, really much nicer, FAR MUCH NICER!

Chapter 5

Germany: Cabaret

RALF AND ULRICH

Next stop, *schönes liebes Deutschland!*

After arriving at the airport in Hamburg, I got on the S-Bahn without having to run my ticket through a machine, as you do in most metros. Would this system work in any country other than law-abiding Germany?

My first hosts in Hamburg were another couple, Ralf and Ulrich. Their flat was located near the Altona station on a street lined with elegant nineteenth century buildings. I assumed this area had been far enough from the city center to escape war-time bombing. I hauled myself and my luggage up the four flights of stairs. Ralf was in his early forties, with a shock of strong-looking black hair and prominent teeth. He told me that Ulrich was still at work. Their apartment was spacious, with Art Nouveau stucco work running around the edges of the ceilings. I had my own room, one that served as the couple's office. I welcomed this after two living room stays.

"Would you like to rest or go out with me?" Ralf asked.

"I'm in Hamburg for the first time," I smiled, "so of course I'd like to go out."

Ralf took his bike and got one for me from a stand of rental bikes near the station. As we rode along, I remarked what a nice neighborhood he lived in. "Yes," he said, "but the rents and housing prices are going up. Ulrich and I can't afford to buy anything here." Ralf rode me past the Altona Rathaus where he and Ulrich had tied the knot in a civil ceremony a few months earlier. He pointed out the back door, where other newlyweds had left champagne bottles and scattered rice.

Down to the Elbe and along the waterfront. On the opposite shore stretched the port, with docks, cranes, some wind turbines revolving their blades. "Hamburg is the second largest port in Europe," Ralf told me. "People are at work there around the clock." I thought, Of course the clever Germans figured out how to make their ports thrive while those in other countries aren't doing as well.

As we approached the city center, Ralf pointed out the Elbphilharmonie, a huge new glass and steel structure being built atop an old brick warehouse on the tip of an island. According to Ralf, construction had been delayed when the city said the design wasn't safe, the old building couldn't support the new one; then the problems were resolved. "I think it will be a great new symbol of the city," Ralf said, "the new Hamburg rising on top of the old."

Through HafenCity. Ralf told me this was the largest inner-city development project in Europe. I was glad we were seeing it on bikes, since like most modern buildings, the ones here required only bike-speed inspection, not foot-speed. The design and the materials used in their construction were superior to anything I'd seen in other parts of Europe. The Germans!

Ralf waited obediently at all traffic lights. When I contrasted this with the British and American way, he said seriously, "Suppose a child saw us go against the light. That would set a bad example."

To the Rathaus, where Ulrich joined us on his bike; Ralf had been keeping him posted about our movements with his mobile. Ulrich was tall, thickly built, with small eyes, small mouth, and a bristle of black and gray hair. Ulrich had lived in England for a year, and Ralf had told me Ulrich's English was better than his own. My sense of Ulrich's superior English wasn't immediate. Ralf seemed able to say almost everything he wanted to, if given some time to find words and piece phrases together.

That evening, I accompanied Ralf and Ulrich as they met up with Ralf's brother and sister-in-law in a tapas restaurant to watch a football match, Hamburg versus Freiburg. We sat in a row at a long table. This made sense in terms of watching the game on the screen on the other side of the room, less sense in terms of conversation. Almost the only talk I had with the sister-in-law, sitting on the other side of Ralf, was to ask about her background, since she didn't look typically German. She said, "I'm from Iran. I used to live in Freiburg, so I'm rooting for both teams." Ralf held a Hamburg flag in his lap, extended over the laps of his brother and sister-in-law. When neither side scored a goal for much of the game, I joked that Hamburg wasn't scoring because he didn't wave his flag enough. I liked Ralf's attitude toward the game and our watching it, which had an edge of humor.

A televised football match wouldn't have been my first choice for a communal experience, yet I could understand how the crowd in the restaurant enjoyed responding as a unit, in dismay or relief. I liked that the man sitting in front of us made some cheerful remark to Ulrich about their similar jackets. I pictured us all in a rathskeller, linking arms, singing songs, swinging beer mugs. At last Hamburg scored one goal, which was enough to secure victory. People jumped up, whooped. A couple kissed.

Saturday morning, we had breakfast in the dining room. There were almost as many different kinds of cheese as breads, though the rolls weren't as tasty or as different from each other as I'd imagined, buying them at the *Bäckerei* under Ulrich's supervision.

Ralf told me the typical Hamburger was cold and un-friendly. "Germans who move here from the South complain about it." Ulrich: "The saying is, If you go to a bar in Cologne, you'll hear someone's life story within five minutes. If you die in Hamburg, it may take five years before someone notices." This derived from an incident in which a man had lain dead in his apartment for five years before the police investigated, and then only because a neighbor complained the man wasn't cleaning the area before his front door, as required. Both Ralf and Ulrich were from the Hamburg area, and I said, "You two prove that the stereotype that all Hamburgers are unfriendly just isn't true."

By now, I'd identified Ralf as the sweet, even-tempered one in the couple, Ulrich as potentially more testy. I worried a little that Ulrich would become truly annoyed about some-thing, maybe me. However, he never crossed the line. The closest I came to annoying him was when Ralf explained that Ulrich's responsibility was to make their lunches since he him-self usually did the grocery shopping and made dinner. "Well, he should make you lunch in that case," I said. Ulrich gave me a mildly dirty look.

I spoke some German when I could find the words, mostly with sweet Ralf, and he was encouraging. I'd taken a few semesters of German at college, and my ability to speak the language a little was like a gift I'd created for myself long ago, hidden away, then sometimes stumbled across in later years.

Ulrich said he and Ralf had things to do in the afternoon. I was happy to go off by myself. I sat on a swing in a park nearby. This was the first moment in which I could be alone and think, "My German adventure has begun." I was excited, curious, though also "in for it." I was roaming about in a country where I had only a rudimentary grasp of the language. Trying to find the river, I became disoriented and asked a man which way it was. I got through at least that brief exchange in German. When a ferry arrived at the Docklands stop, I asked another man if it went to Blankenese. Not understanding his response, I had to ask if he spoke English. Thankfully he did. He said he didn't think the ferry went that far, showing me a map on the wall.

The ferry glided past Ovelgönne, with its pretty villas among green trees, its sand beach which had more the look of a beach on the sea. As a Californian, I wasn't used to beaches on big rivers. Turning around and looking at the other bank of the Elbe, it was a shock to see such an entirely different world of docked ships and cranes and stacked containers. The ferry didn't in fact go to Blankenese, making its last stop at Finkenwerder, then returning upriver.

I got off near the Speicherstadt district of old brick warehouses bordering canals. I was impressed by how many of these warehouses had survived the war, though a photograph on a placard showed there used to be many more. This was the Hamburg I'd read about years before in Christopher Isherwood's *Down There on a Visit*. This novel formed one of my few points of reference for the city. Still, this little was more than I had in some places I'd visited. I needed such points of reference to enjoy a place fully. They were like translucent sheets covered with colored designs that I could lay over my vision of the real place. Embarrassing to admit but, when I'd walked around Copenhagen for the first time several years ago, I'd been eager to find some clips from *Hans Christian Andersen* with Danny Kaye. I couldn't help feeling that the brightly colored Hollywood sets would enrich my experience.

One of my transparencies for Germany as a whole was *Cabaret*. This musical crystallized for me and perhaps many other non-Germans our view of the country between the wars. Decadent Weimar-ians at the start of the story gave way to grim fascists at the end. I'd bought *Berlin Stories* in a used bookstore in Tel Aviv and read it on the flight from Paris. I found there a different Sally Bowles, English rather than American, minorly talented rather than majorly like Liza Minnelli. Thinking back to the film version of the musical, I realized that, for all its air of being more realistic than the typical old-fashioned sort, it created an implausibility of why someone as talented as Liza Minnelli couldn't find a better gig than the small divey Kit Kat Club. In the original story, the whole point of Sally was that she wasn't talented enough to hit it big, whereas you had no doubt Liza would go on to greater things.

Cabaret figured in most people's minds as a movie. I preferred another *Cabaret*, the scrappy little production staged by a traveling company in my home town in the summer after my junior year in high school. My piano teacher, Mrs. Vinson, was always trying to get me to accompany singers and musicians, and it was thanks to her that I got a call from Aiden, the director-manager-whatnot of the company, asking if I would play for them. Something had happened to the original accompanist – illness, departure, death, I don't recall, and maybe I never knew. The show opened in two days.

Although I wasn't a very good pianist, skating through many years of lessons without much preparation had left me with some skill at sight-reading. I called on this to stagger through a couple of rehearsals, then a ghastly opening night. Sitting on stage afterward and telling the assembled cast just how ghastly it was, Aiden turned to me. "Gary, all the songs dragged. You *must* get those tempos up." I only nodded, turning red, without reminding him that the night before, he'd warned me, "When the tempos drag, the singers blame the accompanist."

Predictably, I'd become instantly smitten with Aiden, in part because he'd rested his leg against mine while we had our first – and as it turned out only – conversation alone together. I later figured out he was romantically involved with Hannah, the girl playing Sally. However, I was at an age when logical considerations didn't stop the crush from crushing in. Riding my bike home after the night of the leg touching, curving back and forth across the empty street, I thought of the divine Aiden wearing the world of the theater around his shoulders like a sparkling magic cape. I sang one of the songs from the show to myself, "Maybe This Time." Maybe for once things would work out, after so many disappointments, and I would find romance.

JÖRG

A couple of days later, saying goodbye to Ralf and Ulrich, I moved on to another host, Jörg, who lived in Eimsbüttel, north of the city center. Jörg solved the Couchsurfing problem of how a guest could arrive during the day while the host was at work. He told me he would leave keys for me under the cover of his bicycle seat, a black bike with a blue seat, though I had a moment of doubt when I found two black bikes with blue seat covers parked in front of his building. Opening the door of his apartment, I was greeted by a note from Jörg lying in the hall.

Jörg didn't arrive home until ten. He was short, bearded. He had a pleasant voice, his r's turning to w's so that he sounded like Elmer Fudd. While he said funny things, the humor was conveyed solely by his words, not his dead-pan face. This was my father's style, which probably helped me attune to it more quickly than some people. Jörg told me he used to be much fatter (gummy bears were a particular temptation). He still had a substantial pot belly. He rubbed it at times, showing the ambivalent attitude we men had toward our stomachs: though we believed they should be flat, there was something we liked about having them stick out. Maybe their kinship with the sticking-out phallus.

In emails from back home, several friends had said they understood what guests were getting out of the Couchsurfing experience, but what about the hosts? I replied that most hosts were extroverts, with exceptions like Ralf and Ulrich, or Gershem and Zelik in Tel Aviv. Jörg was a typical host who liked to talk. With me sitting on the small couch and Jörg in a folding chair he'd placed across from me, he proceeded to talk for several hours.

Jörg had different views from Ralf about several aspects of Hamburg. Ralf had showed me HafenCity with pride. Jörg, by contrast, told me the original design had contained lots of parks and public spaces the city later eliminated, realizing it could make more money by increasing the building density. "The city has only built one school there so far, and it put the playground on the roof to avoid using land it could tax." Either flexible in my thoughts or easily swayed, I at once saw the development in a different light, describing it as "soulless."

Jörg was even more scathing on the subject of the Elbphilharmonie, which he claimed was a pharaonic vanity project initiated by a former city mayor. "Yes, all projects like this go over budget, but this one has set some kind of record" – or "wecord," as he pronounced it. "Once it's finished, it will cost so much money to maintain that even if it's sold out every day for the next two hundred years, it will still be in debt." I reflected that it would make for interesting travel if, in every place I visited, I could choose two hosts who would present diametrically opposite views this way.

Jörg showed me where I would be sleeping, in a room beyond the dining area. I found he'd laid pamphlets and maps of the city all over the bed, like a banner saying, "Welcome to Hamburg!"

After seeing more of the center the next day, I took the S-Bahn to the affluent riverside suburb of Blankenese, which I'd missed earlier. I had a fondness for affluent turn-of-the-century German suburbs, the ample charming houses, which looked like they would be comfortable to live in. On the slopes above the Elbe, I had a pleasant ramble up and down and along the many public paths and stairways. A huge cargo ship passed on the steel-gray river, heading for the North Sea.

In the evening, Jörg secured one of the city bikes for me, and we rode to Sternschanze to the south. This district was once working class, he explained, smelling of the nearby slaughterhouses. Later it had attracted counterculture types and drug dealers. In a city with a very tight housing market, the movement lately was toward gentrification, with chains like Starbucks trying to elbow their way in. Jörg pointed out the rolling metal doors covering the front of a chi chi new eyeglass shop. "They need those to keep angry local people from smashing the windows." Sternschanze was the most appealing part of the city I'd seen so far, with lovely old buildings and an arty edge. "I'm getting to see it at just the right moment," I told Jörg. "After it's been fixed up a little, though before it gets too commercialized."

Jörg showed me the Rota Flora, a notorious squat in an old theater. It looked partway toward becoming a ruin, with most of its decoration worn away like old cake icing and the whole building covered with graffiti. A sheltered area in front contained mattresses where homeless people could sleep. One already had an occupant. This was one of the few places in the city where the police didn't dare roust the homeless, Jörg said. With a rare smile, he told me, "I give money to the collective. It relieves my guilt at working for an advertising company, which is part of the capitalist world."

We had dinner at a Chinese restaurant. As we ate, Jörg asked if I was writing about my travels. I told him I was working on a collection of short stories set in some of the places I'd visited. "Maybe you could write a book about Couchsurfing," he suggested. No, I said without even thinking about the idea. This was before Vienna and *Gustav Klimt: das Musical*.

On the ride home, the lights from Jörg's bicycle and mine kept merging on the sidewalk ahead of us as we shifted them to the left or right. The interweaving lights gave me a sense of us as intimates.

TOBIAS

On to Lübeck. The sight of the famous Holstentor ahead of me, with copper church spires rising behind it, made me hope this city would provide some of the escape-into-the-past charm I craved in European traveling. The old city center occupied a large island, with the Trave flowing around it. Lübeck had been bombed during the war, like most German cities, though not as badly as some. I walked along the west side of the island. The house of my host, Tobias, was on a beautiful spot, with only a quiet street and a strip of lawn separating it from the water. Wash hung on a clothes line that stood on the lawn strip, a homey touch.

Tobias's messages to me had been long, numerous, and sometimes strange. In one, he asked if there was something about gay people that made them not leave references for their hosts: the one other gay surfer who'd stayed with him hadn't written him a reference. He also asked if all gay people were thin and fit like this other man. He himself was too fond of good food for that, he wrote. I went so far as to ask myself whether I should find a different host. Yet while some things made me doubtful about Tobias, I appreciated his proposing some activities we might do together during my visit. And by writing to me at such length, I had more of an idea of who he was than I usually did before meeting a host.

Tobias was stout, round-faced, with hair and beard almost completely white. The house, which I'd taken for an old one, turned out to have been built only thirty years ago. Tobias showed me his wife's room on the second floor. This had a demented Miss Havisham look, if Miss Havisham had been a scholar. Books and papers were chaotically heaped on the floor and completely covered a desk. Wherever they lay, they gathered a coating of dust. Tobias said his wife was writing a thesis, though it was difficult for me to imagine her getting any work done here. "It's too bad she has this room, since she's hardly ever here," he said. "It's the best one in the house, with a view of the river."

The room where I would sleep was on the top floor. Tobias was an accumulator, like his wife, and this room was filled with car magazines, *Berlinale* programs. They also seemed to share a lack of sensitivity about how things looked. The whole house had the appearance of a storehouse, a mere repository of various stuff.

Tobias mentioned there was a *Musikhochschule* near his house, a music school. When I asked whether it gave concerts, he said he wasn't sure, he wasn't that interested in classical music. I asked what he thought of the Kunsthalle in Hamburg, and he said he wasn't very interested in art either. I'd come to Germany partly out of cultural interest, then found the people I met here didn't necessarily share my enthusiasm. Tobias was more keen on watching a soccer match scheduled for that evening.

About to enter the bathroom the next morning, I heard Tobias downstairs on the telephone with his wife, whom he spoke with in French, their shared language. He referred to me as "*l'Américain gai*," then lowered his voice as if to say something he didn't want overheard. I continued into the bathroom. If he is saying something bad about me, I thought, I don't want to know.

I hurried out to buy some food. However, while cafes were in plentiful supply, stores where I could get groceries were not. The best I could do was a store where I bought fruits and vegetables and Turkish yogurt, no cereal. We had a breakfast of yogurt and fruit and soft-boiled eggs that Tobias prepared, kept warm by small cloth hoods.

One of Lübeck's claims to fame was as the home town of Thomas Mann. I set off with Tobias to the Buddenbrookhaus for the press opening of an exhibit about Mann's youngest daughter, Elisabeth Mann Borgese. Several people spoke in turn while a couple of journalists took notes and Tobias made a sound recording, holding out a microphone. Tobias worked for a community radio station. Unable to understand anything except an occasional flash of German, I was left to notice things like what people wore (the male speakers, sharp suits, while Tobias, who had told me he didn't like to shop, was content with a plaid flannel shirt). After the speeches, Tobias explained to me who the people were: the young woman who had created the exhibit, the director of the museum, whom I idly daydreamed about as potential husband material. All of Tobias's big belly shook when he laughed, talking with people.

That evening, Tobias made a tasty dinner of chicken and fried eggplant with pasta. He smacked his lips while he ate. It seemed clear he was eating without any attempt to limit himself. For dessert, lemon sorbet with some of the strawberries I'd bought.

I got Tobias onto the subject of his wife. They'd met in their early twenties in Barcelona. Tobias was hanging out in a park hoping to connect with someone who would put him up after a bad night in a hostel; a bad night that included getting approached by "a homosexual." He met Maria. By the second night of staying with her and her flatmate, he was sleeping with Maria. They lived first in Barcelona, then Toulouse. Tobias moved to Lübeck for his radio job. Maria, coming with him, was bored here. "She was studying Catalan literature and got tired of people asking things like, Is Catalan a language or a dialect?" A few years ago, she got a job in Palma de Mallorca. Recently, because of the economic crisis in Spain, she lost this job and was now unemployed like almost all her friends, who were mainly academics or in the arts. She returned to Lübeck every few months. "I wish she'd come back permanently," Tobias said with a sad expression.

I accompanied Tobias to an outdoor market in the morning, paying for most of the food he picked out. I looked at the labels on the fruits and vegetables to improve my German vocabulary and paid attention to what Tobias said to the stallholders. I noted how he told them, "*Ich hätte gern*" when asking for something.

Tobias gave me a tour of Lübeck. First, to a *Flohmarkt*, a flea market, beside a church. We ate slices of rhubarb tart, sitting with several people Tobias knew. A couple of them sang in the church choir. They were pleasant and jolly, not the Serious Germans I'd sometimes encountered, and they spoke more or less good English.

Later, we attended an open house of twenty-odd non-profit organizations in the city. While out back in the garden, a male chorus sang and children got their faces painted, Tobias and I wandered through a large room filled with displays set up by the organizations. I lingered at a stand for the Fritz Reuter Gesellschaft. I was tickled by its slight nuttiness, with acolytes tending the shrine of someone I assumed was only a minor figure in German literature. (I know that by writing this, I leave myself open to ridicule from people who are better informed.) Tobias talked with the man and woman briefly, then walked off. I examined an immense three volume collection of Herr Reuter's letters, wondering if they were dull. The man talked on and on to me in German. I could understand the gist of what he said as he showed me different parts of the book, but had no idea how to respond until "*sehr interessant*" popped into my mind and rolled off my tongue: "very interesting."

At times, I had an impulse to set off on my own, having become used to the role of lone explorer. By the end of the day, it was clear I'd been much better off sticking with Tobias. I might have missed the musty interior of an old church or two, yet I'd gotten a taste of the interior life of the city, which was more interesting. In fact, *sehr interessant*.

Another Couchsurfer in Lübeck I'd written to, Sarah, couldn't host me, but suggested we at least meet while I was in town. At Tobias's suggestion, I asked her over for dinner this evening. Sarah was a few years younger than I, slender, rather attractive, with thick dark hair threaded with gray. I felt like a quasi-host, taking her coat and purse.

The three of us sat on the bench in front of the house, peeling and cutting up vegetables. An occasional neighbor passed, greeting Tobias. This is pleasant, I thought; homey, non-touristic. Sarah said she liked helping her host make a meal. "I studied in China when I was younger, and if someone invites you to dinner there, you're expected to help with the preparations."

Sarah had married an Italian man she met in China. She returned to Europe while he stayed on. "He kept saying he would join me soon, when he'd finished his research in a few months, then a few more months. Finally after two years of 'I'm coming home soon,' I divorced him. Maybe he's still in China and still doing his research. I don't know." Twelve years ago, Sarah had moved from Berlin to Lübeck, wanting to live somewhere smaller and quieter. She'd rented an apartment outside the old city. She'd considered living in the same neighborhood Tobias did, but hadn't wanted to deal with the seasonal flooding of the river.

Over dinner, I found Sarah odd and difficult. She soon mounted the hobbyhorse of Eckhart Tolle, eager to spread his ideas. She put questions to Tobias about his wife that I wouldn't have asked until I'd known someone longer. She did apologize for being "nosy," a word we had to explain to Tobias. Viewing his situation from astride her hobbyhorse, Sarah told Tobias, "You shouldn't see your wife's decision to live in Spain as an attack on you. She's only looking after herself, doing what she needs to do."

Sarah was even more challenging when Tobias said he liked shopping at City, a large supermarket on the outskirts of town. "You should support the small local shops," she scolded. Recalling how few local shops I'd been able to find, I wondered if I should hold Tobias partly to blame for this. . . . Tobias kept talking about "we" out of marital habit: we think this, we like that. Poor Tobias, he missed his Señora Havisham.

Sarah had introduced herself to Tobias as Lotte when they met, which I found puzzling. Later, she explained that "Sarah" was a name she used only on Couchsurfing and similar sites. She worried about having information about her gathered from the internet. I didn't like the multiple names, this suggestion of slight paranoia.

There was lots of talk about food, with the two locals comparing views on restaurants in town. Continuing her pattern of provocation, Sarah-Lotte made some remark about Tobias eating too much, never being satisfied, though again acknowledging this wasn't her business. Thankfully Tobias took this in his stride.

In the midst of one of Tobias's long stories, Sarah rose, put on her coat, and took up her purse. Tobias talked on as if he didn't see she was ready to leave.

Sarah and I agreed to meet the following day, though after our rather bumpy dinner, I was dubious about spending more time with her. In the event, as we walked around town, I found her more enjoyable. With Tobias, she had to force her philosophy down a not very willing throat, whereas I obligingly spoke her language. Yes, we should live in the present, not worry about things we couldn't control, ask the universe for what we wanted. At the Heiligen-Geist-Hospital, looking at the tiny rooms in which old people used to finish out their days, with space for little more than a single bed and a washstand,

I said, "I could probably live in one of these." Sarah smiled approvingly. "Your needs must be simple," she said.

Sarah gave me three options for a car trip, to the north, the south, or the east. I selected the last, partly because, though she said the choice was mine, I sensed she believed this was the best option. She'd only had her little VW Golf for two weeks and apologized for her slow, careful driving. I said, "You drive the way I would drive if I drove." Sarah said she liked this sentence and wrote it down in her notebook.

We traveled through a rolling landscape of wheat fields and fragments of woodland. Big old trees lined the road in places. Here and there, we had glimpses of the pewter Baltic Sea. Sarah pointed out an abandoned guard tower, showing we'd crossed into the former East. The homes and villages we passed were quite spruce. Sarah had grown up as an East German, and I asked if this area looked different from the way it had under the Communists. Oh yes, she said.

We had lunch on the terrace of a restaurant in the village of Klütz. Sarah told me to order for us, to practice my German. I tried out, "*Wir hätten gern . . .*" On to Schloss Bothmer. The Schloss veiled by scaffolding, the park almost unrecognizable since her last visit, Sarah said. It was now cleared of underbrush, though also, she felt, of much of its charm. The Schloss had been allowed to moulder under the East German government and at present was being brought back to life by the unified Germany.

I felt sleepy on the drive back. Sarah talked on and on, sometimes repeating things she'd said before. About "making a prayer to the universe," for one thing. I asked if you should say the prayer aloud, repeat it, write it down. No, Sarah said, none of that was necessary. "The only thing to be careful about is making the prayer specific. Otherwise you may get your wish granted in a bad form."

Drowsily, I ran through the plot of "The Monkey's Paw" in my mind. The enchanted paw granted three wishes. When a man used it to ask for two hundred pounds, his son was killed at the factory where he worked and the man received in compensation – two hundred pounds. The man's wife insisted he make a second wish to call their son back to life, another wish unfortunately lacking in specificity, in this case the addition of ". . . exactly as he was before the accident and a week buried in a coffin."

A good thing the man had a third wish left with which to cancel the second before it was too late.

DANIEL

After I'd bought my train ticket to Cologne, my host there, Daniel, told me he wouldn't get home until nine, leaving me with a couple of hours to kill. A succession of surprises in that the train station had a luggage storage area, it was affordable, and I managed to squeeze my big suitcase and shoulder bag into the space provided. This left me free to explore.

I emerged from the station to find the cathedral just across a plaza. Photographs of Cologne after the war showed the city half-obliterated, but the cathedral by some miracle intact in its basic structure, the twin towers still soaring. The cathedral always dark in these images, as if roasted on a spit, the city around it crumbling like softened honeycomb and oddly pale, with the paleness of ash. According to one source, the mundane explanation why the cathedral had survived was that it was such a convenient landmark for Allied bombers searching for Cologne, they avoided hitting it directly. Today the stone of the cathedral was still blackened, as if the fires that had consumed the city had occurred only recently.

Daniel lived fairly far outside the center, on the other side of the Rhine, though his neighborhood looked equally post-war. Cologne didn't seem like Hamburg, where you came to intact older neighborhoods farther out. Daniel was lean, rather attractive. He mentioned he was from Australia. I said, "And here I was thinking your English was amazingly good for a German, and that you must have learned it in Australia." He kept referring to Australia as Oz, which bothered me a little. It was like Sarah having another name, creating some confusion in my mind.

Daniel's father had been German, expelled from the Sudetenland following the war and resentful ever after. Daniel had lived in Germany since his late twenties, though I didn't get an explanation of why he preferred it to Australia. He taught English here, in a good post. The school where he worked "shoves money up my ass," as he said in his earthy way. His tanned face, too, had the look of the earth. He had a habit of running a hand over his whole face or just the lower half, though I couldn't see what motivated this physically – that he itched? It appeared more like the result of excessive energy.

Daniel talked about the benefits he received from meditating. I said, "I spent six months living at the Zen Center in San Francisco. I enjoyed meditating when I lived there, but I stopped as soon as I left."

"You seem like a calm person, so you probably don't need it as much," Daniel said. He talked about a Thich Nhat Hanh book he was reading; how he tried to leave a small "footprint." He avoided flying because it was so damaging to the environment. "When I'm on the point of doing something, I consider what effect it would have if millions of other people in the world did it, too."

"I'd think that would paralyze you from doing much of anything," I said.

In his profile, Daniel had mentioned he had a girlfriend, Jana. When he accepted my request to host, he told me that he and Jana had broken up. Now I learned this had happened only a month ago. Daniel had just moved out of the larger bedroom, the one I would occupy and he would soon rent, and relocated to the loft bedroom. Jana had gotten involved with a man from work who was closer to her own age, while Daniel was sixteen year older. Continuing my survey of how people in couples met, I put this question to Daniel. "She was one of my students," he admitted. "Though in my defense, I'll point out that I did wait until after the end of the school year before asking for her telephone number."

Trying to get back into the dating scene, a week ago Daniel had gone on a blind date with a friend of a friend. He'd found the woman attractive. He told me how her tight clothes and stuck-out boobs had brought sex at once into the picture. Although she'd said a couple of flirtatious things in text messages after the first date, so far she'd put off having a second.

"I'm getting tired of exchanging long messages with her," Daniel said. "I still haven't answered her last one."

I said, "When I'm in that situation, I send a message that just says, 'Okay.' That way, you have responded, but you're also communicating, 'I don't want more chatting back and forth.'" Daniel said he liked this idea and sent the woman the "Okay" message.

Daniel drank a non-alcoholic beer with a shot of raspberry syrup out of a typically tall German glass. "I stopped drinking alcohol at fifteen. By then, I'd already had enough experience of getting drunk to know it was bad for me."

Daniel asked me some questions about myself, including what motivated me to write, whether I'd had much sex while traveling. I suspected Daniel would talk to me more explicitly about sex if we got to know each other better.

"You're gay, aren't you?" When I said I was, Daniel went on, "I understand sex is easier to find in the gay world."

"Probably, but sometimes I think it ends up being more a matter of quantity than quality."

Not feeling I needed to spend much more time exploring central Cologne, in the morning I set off for the suburb of Brühl to see Schloss Augustusburg, which Ralf had recommended. At Neumarkt Station, I dealt with a pleasant, slow-talking woman at a ticket window. When I said I wanted to go to Schloss Augustusburg, she gave a veritable gasp of approval at my choice. She ended up selling me a day ticket that covered both Cologne and Bonn.

After seeing the Schloss, I continued on to Bonn farther south. This city looked agreeable only by comparison with even less agreeable Cologne. Returning to Cologne, I still had enough energy left to make another circuit in the center. After a while, realizing the mainly post-war buildings weren't going to give me any pleasure, I focused on the people. They weren't very prepossessing either, generally homely and dowdy. The city was living down to my lowest expectations. Cologne seemed to have essentially vanished during the war, replaced by bland, nondescript New Cologne, an almost entirely different city. It didn't surprise me that Daniel had said he wasn't very interested in old buildings. Who would choose to live in New Cologne if he were?

Dinner with Daniel. "Are you any good in the kitchen?" he asked. "I can cut things up and take instructions," I replied. Fortunately he'd chosen to make that most fool-proof of dishes, pasta, with a salad of greens from his allotment. Daniel dished up first from the bowl, and I took the pasta that remained. When Daniel quickly (as someone who does everything quickly) finished his pasta, I began to doubt I'd taken only half; maybe I'd taken more. Certainly more than I wanted in the end. "Would you like the rest of this?" I said, offering him the pasta left on my plate. "I wondered where the rest had gone," he joked, looking at the bowl. Daniel made frequent references to the idea of Acceptance, and I hoped this included his accepting that I might have been a little greedy.

More stories from Daniel followed, mostly about his love life. A recurring figure in these was the woman who thrust her boobs toward him. Daniel cast himself as the "what else could I do but have sex with her" victim. Even if he made what might be seen as the first move, as with asking Jana for her number, this was prefaced by the woman sending out sexual signals, thrusting her boobs toward him in provocation.

Daniel had children by two mothers, one French and the other German. In both cases, it was the woman who had "lured" him into involvement. He'd met the French woman at a WWOOFer farm in Australia. "After I walked her to her tent, she invited me in," Daniel told me. "What else could that mean, to invite a man into your tent late at night?"

Daniel's daughter from the French woman was fourteen and lived in a village in the South of France. He communicated with Caroline in French, though his French was limited and this was becoming more of a problem as she grew older. The other daughter, Trudi, lived in a suburb of Cologne. Her mother was what Daniel described as a "professional mother," who made money by raising, in addition to Trudi, three foster kids and two she'd had with her ex-husband.

In a possibly meaningless parallel, the French woman, who had never married, had adopted a Colombian boy. In a couple of weeks, Caroline would make the trip up to Paris on her own for the first time with her adopted brother, and Daniel would meet them and accompany them to Cologne.

He was arranging activities for the two sets of children, who had met before.

Daniel said he was going to bed. I said, "I just had the same thought. You see, after only a couple of days together, we're already getting synchronized."

NIKLAS AND MILENA

On to Darmstadt and from there to Basel. In both places, I stayed with friends, two halves of a couple in a long-distance relationship. I'll flip the calendar pages forward to my arrival in Constance, on the southern border of Germany. As a reader, I'm grateful when a writer tells me about some things in detail and even more grateful when he skips over others entirely.

My hosts in Constance were Niklas, a German (Swabian, to be precise), and his wife Milena, a Pole. Milena maybe ten years younger than Niklas, though I didn't take in the age difference until much later, when she mentioned it. My awareness of this was obscured by Niklas still being much younger than I was and by my finding him rather sexy, with his broad shoulders and well-developed arms revealed by a polo shirt. Niklas was also the main conversationalist in the couple, with a dry sense of humor. Milena said several times that her English wasn't good, though when she did talk, it seemed fine. Niklas would even consult her when he couldn't think of a word, as if her English were actually better. More surprisingly, Niklas told me he would seek her advice about his written German, since thanks to his Swabian upbringing, his was less correct. Their respective degrees of talkativeness appeared more a matter of temperament than language skills.

Constance was so jammed up against Switzerland, one end of the train station was on Swiss soil. Thanks to the difficulty of bombing it during the war without risk of damage to neutral Switzerland, Constance was that rarity, an intact ancient German city. The building where the couple lived was old from my perspective, late nineteenth century, though relatively new for the city. Niklas, an architect, told me he'd always wanted to live in this particular building. Later, they'd found an apartment there. It was on the top floor, which had required hauling my suitcase up six flights of stairs; I'd joked to Niklas that I never chose a host who lived on the ground floor. The apartment was modernized, though with big raw-cut beams running through some of the walls and picturesque views out to quaint steep roofs and a church tower.

Two parakeets occupied a cage in the main room where we ate and where my bed was located. I'd always considered a bird a fairly pointless pet. Still, I did enjoy their cheeping and hopping around, and they gave the three of us – and probably Niklas and Milena when alone – something fun to talk about. Blue Boy had a mix of yellow and green feathers (the misapprehension that he was blue caused by the couple buying him in the evening, when they couldn't see his color clearly). The other was pure yellow; his name, Żółty, meant "yellow" in Polish. Blue Boy was aggressive, Żółty shyer. The top of the cage was left open, and sometimes the birds would come out. Only Blue Boy would actually fly, while Żółty would drop to the floor and have to be returned to the cage on a finger. Blue Boy would play a game with Niklas in which the bird picked up his ring from the palm of his hand.

Milena made dinner, refusing my offer of help. Niklas questioned me about my writing. I explained how I'd written one story, all the different strands of experience that combined to form it. "It was like a place at the edge of a stream where lots of twigs and leaves and other odds and ends come together."

I made allusions to my gay status a few times, then stopped when neither responded to these.

Niklas and Milena had first encountered each other in a pen pal chat room while Milena was still living in Poland. They'd corresponded for a year, never expecting to meet in person. Then they both visited Spain at the same time and romance blossomed. Niklas wanted to learn Polish. Several times, he referred to the "funny way" one said things in this language.

Niklas worked at an architectural firm just across the border in Switzerland. He said he and his colleagues passed the day largely in silence, in contrast to the German firm where he used to work. He found this oppressive. "In the German firm when it was getting near Christmas, people would stop working so hard. What point was there in starting a new project then? In the Swiss firm, Christmas coming closer makes people work even harder because they think, 'Oh, we have to wrap everything up.'"

Niklas considered the Swiss "more German than the Germans." He told a story to illustrate this. "I like to bike over the border to run in a park on the Swiss side. Usually I just cross the border, no problem. But one day guards were checking passports at one of the crossings. I told them I didn't have mine, and they wouldn't let me through. So I used another crossing. Then to be a little – " getting the word from Milena – " a little provocative, I rode my bike past the first crossing. The guards chased after me and fined me fifty Swiss francs. When I said this wasn't right, they handcuffed me and held me in a cell for a couple of hours. I had to sit there in my running clothes."

Niklas said he wasn't sure he wanted to go on working as an architect. He complained about one of his current projects, to build a house for a wealthy Swiss couple. "The wife wants it to have six bathrooms, though only two people live there. And even when she gets her house with six bathrooms, that won't make her any happier." Niklas joked about becoming what I called a *Haus-mann*, staying at home while Milena worked, a scenario that seemed unlikely to come true. Milena had almost finished a degree in Russian literature, but lamented she had no idea what to do in terms of work. She'd recently taken a sales job at a clothing store.

My sleep that night somewhat disturbed by the chiming of the two nearby church clocks every quarter hour. At least the birds, under their cover, were silent.

Niklas gone by the time I got up in the morning. This left me to have breakfast with Milena, the one in the couple I had less rapport with. However, some questions from me dug up an engrossing, though hair-raising story from her about working as an au pair in England at nineteen. The couple employing her got divorced in the midst of her stay, and the story included the wife, who was from the Philippines, stabbing her English husband on a camping trip.

I rented a bike and rode to the island of Mainau. A storm hit in the afternoon, by which time I'd returned to Constance. Milena had told me she would be home from work at three. Despite our getting along well enough during our breakfast together, my instinct was still to minimize the contact of one shy person with another, and I aimed to arrive closer to six, when Niklas would return. I read in a cafe, drinking a mug of hot chocolate by sipping up one spoonful at a time.

I took Niklas and Milena out to dinner, then we walked around, the rain having stopped. Niklas played tour guide, showing me things like the narrowest building in the city and the spot where Jan Hus was burned at the stake. I pointed to a house I liked, with Rococo frothing around the windows.

"Niklas, could you build me a house like that?" I asked.

"Yes," he said, "though I would discourage the idea. The style of that house is from the past. It's better to build a house in the current style."

"But then there wouldn't be any decoration," I complained.

"Decoration is expensive."

"The Swiss have money. Can't they afford decoration?"

I walked beside Niklas, talking mostly with him, Milena saying little. Sometimes they spoke together in the lowered, intimate voices of a couple. They seemed very interwoven, a "good couple" in a way. I conjectured she activated in him some male instinct to protect the younger, less capable female; an instinct that wasn't part of my own makeup. I was pretty sure my friend M., a therapist, would say that Milena was depressed. At the very least, she didn't appear to have a sense of humor, unlike Niklas.

The following day, I couldn't meet my next hosts until the evening – the usual Couchsurfing limitation. I proposed to fill up the morning with a bike ride to Reichenau, another island. Milena had the day off and asked if she could join me. "Of course," I said, though continuing to be doubtful about the shy-plus-shy combination.

Like many shy types, I complained that people didn't draw me out more. During breakfast, Milena asked me questions about my writing and other things. This continued on the bike ride. Answering them made me think, "Maybe I don't actually *like* having to talk a lot. Talking about myself can be boring. After all, there aren't many surprises."

Evidence of Milena's depression accumulated. Their neighbors seemed afraid of Niklas and her, she said, hardly speaking to them. "Projection," I thought. The saddest sign was that she didn't believe the *birds* liked them. "They just pretend to so Niklas and I will take care of them." Milena felt Germans sometimes looked down on her as "another Eastern European bride." The implication was that she'd married Niklas for his more secure financial position as a German. After we returned to town, Milena insisted on accompanying me to the pier and carrying my shoulder bag, which was kind of her.

I made a long boat ride east across Lake Constance to Bregenz at the other end. I sat on a bench running along the port side where the overhang provided shade. The shore slid past from left to right. Some of the slopes were corrugated with green vineyards. The clouds were close overhead, as if we were flying in an airplane. Only this was better than an airplane ride because I was outside and could feel the cool air sweep over me. I took far too many photographs of white sailboats against blue water. One sailboat, two; nearer, farther; turned at this angle or that. Yet each view I snapped promised to be more beautiful than the last.

Cabaret – well, it's never been my favorite musical. It trades charm for cynicism and doesn't take much interest in either romantic life or family life, those two staples of older musicals. I do have happy memories of helping put it on, though. A couple of snippets from my journal tell the story.

The first rehearsal I attended. "'For the dance in 'Sitting Pretty,' Allison whispered urgently, 'play it as fast as you can!' I felt I wasn't playing the piano, but smashing various things on it. Afterward I asked, 'How did it sound?' '*Perfect*,' she said. 'Can you do it that way opening night?' 'Sure,' I said."

The rehearsal the day after the dreadful opening night. "I told Hannah I'd worked on 'Cabaret.' We ran through it. At the end, she crouched beside me, and clapped her hands, and looked at me with big happy eyes. 'That's it, that's marvelous!' I understood how I could be rewarded for my work, just by knowing they need me, and need me to be good."

For a divertissement, a fight erupted between the local dramatic company that leased the theater and Aiden's traveling troupe that was renting it for a month. I'm not sure I ever knew the details of the dispute, but with two parties of a theatrical bent involved, I do recall they put on quite a show. Aiden refused to relinquish his keys to the theater. Molly Jenkins, the local, threatened to call the police and padlock the door. "It was all so wonderful!" I enthused in my journal.

Aiden was like Professor Harold Hill from *The Music Man*, livening up my dull, small town summer with music and theater magic. However, instead of settling down in River City, he and his troupe soon moved on. I wasn't too bereft, for shortly afterward I set off with a group of other teenagers on a five week European Grand Tour. In those days before computer technology and every piece of music under the sun constantly at your fingertips, the driver of our bus had only two cassette tapes at his disposal, and he played them over and over through the speakers. One was the soundtrack to – *Cabaret*. By the end of the first week, as we glided down various European highways, the entire bus-load of students could sing along to the opening song, "*Willkommen*," without missing a word. It provided us with at least a few phrases in German and French we could use during our trip, including "It's nice to meet you" and "Please don't go."

Musicals and traveling rubbed shoulders once again.

Chapter 6

Austria and Italy: Do I Hear a Waltz?

LUKAS AND WOLF

Lukas, my host in Bregenz, had mentioned he lived with his brother, though not that they were identical twins, as I discovered upon my arrival. This was another Couchsurfing first for me, surfing with twins. In fact, the two young men were fairly easy to distinguish physically since Lukas had a wispy mustache while Wolf was clean-shaven. Instead, it was their personalities I found harder to differentiate. They were both soft-spoken, polite. Lukas worked in a bank, Wolf in a health food store.

I tried to see if L&W had anything interesting to say about being twins. People who told me I was a good listener might suppose I listened to be somehow "nice." It was more accurate to say I wanted to be informed and entertained. With the brothers, I mixed direct questions with talk that kept us on the subject; for example, regarding the many movies made about twins. "It would take you a few days to watch all of them," I said. Despite my efforts, L&W didn't say a single interesting thing about their twinness. I guessed Lukas was the older of the two (by a few minutes); he turned out to be the younger. Nothing gave me a sense of their sexuality, aside from Wolf telling a story that started with him sitting on an airplane, hoping a "cheerleader" would sit next to him (instead an old woman did, telling him stories about her life during the war).

I offered to take the brothers out to dinner. "We've already eaten," Lukas said. This worried me, since I was hungry and didn't have any food with me. After a while, Wolf asked if I wanted something to eat, and I had a bowl of Choco Muesli. Munching on this, I asked the brothers how Austrians were different from Germans.

Wolf: "Austrians are more easy-going."

Lukas: "They tend not to move far from home. Most of the people we knew growing up have stayed in this region, the Vorarlberg."

Wolf: "That's true. I can't think of any of them who has moved farther away than Vienna."

I heard about some of the other surfers they'd hosted. The brothers asked surfers to write or draw something on the square pillar in the center of the main room. "You're a writer," Lukas said, "that should be easy for you." I didn't explain to him that this was a form of writing I dreaded. While I could write a novel or a play, guestbooks and things of that kind gave me writer's block.

The next day, I took the cable car up the Pfänder, the mountain behind Bregenz. The complex of buildings at the top was small and homey, with a children's play area and a petting zoo. I was delighted to be up in the Alps and more interested in the eastward view of more mountains than the promoted view west down to the lake. I had a craving for potato chips; bought a big pretzel at one stand since it didn't have any chips; later found chips at another stand. Consuming one chip after another with a steady rhythm, I headed downhill toward the city, taking the longer of two routes offered by orange signposts. I had a pretty descent through the forest, with the sun always more or less ahead of me, so that my view was flooded with light.

In the evening, I followed the brothers downstairs to their storage area, where they had a third bike I could use. I thought I saw their twinness in the easy way they worked together, pumping up the tires. As they rode ahead of me, side by side, the brothers showed a subtle sympathy toward each other in their movements.

We had dinner at a restaurant by the lake, on the terrace. With hosts, I sometimes felt myself assume the guise of a paid companion, like the nameless young woman in *Rebecca*. One of my not very onerous tasks as a companion was to be unfailingly cheerful and positive. I told L&W I thought this restaurant had a better view than the first one we'd tried, which hadn't had a free table. I even went so far as to say I preferred sitting where we were, near the building. "This way you get to see the other people eating, and then the lake." If we had sat closer to the water, I would probably have said how nice it was we didn't have anything blocking our view.

Before I left the following morning, L&W reminded me about writing on the column. Amid all the clever things the non-writers had said, I, the writer, scribbled something lame.

While skipping over several stops in my travels that didn't involve surfing, I'll introduce our next musical. Enthusiasts of all art forms have their favorite little-known works, and enthusiasts of musicals are no exception; in fact, they may lead the pack. One of my ex's wittier remarks was that *House of Flowers* was the world's best-known little-known musical. At the top of my own obscure fav list is *Do I Hear a Waltz?* I borrowed a recording of the cast album from a public library between college terms, liked it (though there was no cymbal crash or bolt of lightning), and marked it in my mind as something I wanted to own one day.

Many years later, I did buy it in its current incarnation as a CD. I got it as a Christmas present for my ex. We had a bad habit of buying "presents" for each other that were in fact things we wanted ourselves. Perhaps suspecting he smelled a selfish rat, his enthusiasm was muted and he didn't play the musical often. I was thankful for this, because after hearing it a few times, I found it almost unbearable. In the odd way that sometimes happened, a work of art had adhered to aspects of my own life and in this case become too emotionally charged. The only way I could approach this musical was through the piano score. If I played one of the songs myself, literally had it in my hands, I felt more in control of this potentially dangerous music. I could make it slower, faster, vary the tone.

Rather than boy-meets-girl, *Waltz?* is middle-aged American woman meets middle-aged (and married) Italian man. They come together while the woman is on holiday in Venice. If there's any happiness in the ending, it consists of the woman taking the advice the Italian gives her in one of his songs, "Take the Moment." Welcome the moment even if it won't last forever, even if a fearful inner voice tells us to say no to it. The woman returns home to Philadelphia PA or wherever she's from and will almost certainly never see the Italian again, though she will treasure his memory.

This story dovetailed with my life in a two-fold way. The first fold. At sixteen, on my Grand Tour, I wandered off by myself during the group's nocturnal whistle stop in Venice and got lost. I was rescued by Giulio, an off-duty Italian policeman, who whisked me away on a madcap adventure that included spending the night at the home of his boyfriend and his boyfriend's unsuspecting father. The next morning, Giulio deposited me back in Piazzale Roma. Over the next couple of years, we exchanged a few letters. "My friend Piero and I are living together now," he wrote in French. "We have a comfortable home where you will always find, in several moments, a room for yourself. All you have to do is get on a plane, and I will take care of the rest." Foolishly, I never managed to get on that plane. In my early twenties, I moved to San Francisco, the capital of the gay world where all my wishes for love and lust would be fulfilled, or so I imagined. I didn't think too often about Giulio in far-off Italy.

The second fold. Thirty years later, I wrote a story about my night with Giulio. The writer writing about his past, particularly one who has a detailed journal to refer to, comes the closest that's humanly possible to time travel. With the incident brought vividly to life again, I regretted never having found my way back to Giulio. Giulio, who had loved my boyishness, my softness, those qualities that had just gone out of fashion in the gay world I entered in my twenties. *Waltz?* got injected into this mix of a past event and my mid-life-crisis rethink about it. In *Waltz?*, I could both relive my Amer-Italian romance and regret its loss from a later vantage point, for the second purpose drawing on the bittersweet quality of the music and the advanced age of the leads. Giulio was telling me that, after taking the first moment, I should have seized another later on.

STEFAN

In Munich, I met up with my friend M. We traveled to Vienna, where, after spending a few days together, he flew to London and I exchanged our hotel room for the apartment of a Viennese host, Stefan. Stefan had warned me his neighborhood was considered a bad one because lots of Turkish people lived there. Although even a "bad neighborhood" in Austria was safe, he said. Walking through it, I added that it was also attractive, with lots of elegant old buildings and scarcely a speck of trash on the streets. I passed Turkish stores, faces; women in full-length black robes, heads covered with scarves.

Crossing a park, I noticed a large sign detailing how people should behave in it. This was written in three languages: German, what I assumed was Turkish, and a third, which appeared Slavic. I'd never seen a sign of this type with so much text, even aside from the triple iterations. Don't use the park as a toilet, don't treat it as a dump and leave old refrigerators and television sets, don't pick the flower (not that there were any flowers in view to pick), don't litter with your Cola bottles and bonbon wrappings. At its most elaborate and from-on-high: "Although kids and young men must sometimes be loud, they must certainly not be so loud that they disturb the old men and the mothers with their babies." I was sure the Viennese joked darkly about "the new Turkish invasion."

On first meeting Stefan, disaster seemed to loom. According to his profile, we had several things in common: we were gay and shared an interest not only in Buddhism, but screwball comedies. In person, Stefan had little to say; I had to generate all the conversation. Although he gave me keys, he appeared reluctant to tell me his schedule that day, as if mistrustful of my intentions. I wondered if he had a job. That wasn't good, a host I couldn't talk with easily and who would also be around a lot. Perhaps he wasn't working because he was ill. He looked ill, enfeebled. Bald head, glasses with dark frames, an attempt to extend the hair on his chin into – I didn't know what exactly, something of interest.

The apartment was spacious, with an entrance hall, living room, two bedrooms. Stefan said he had low rent under rent control. He'd lived in the apartment for fifteen years, and his sister had lived here before him. Asian-style furniture and bric-a-brac spoke of his interest in the East. The rooms were filled with plants, in pots, baskets, raised on podiums, placed on shelves, on window sills. The plants were vital, contrasting with Stefan's lack of vitality, and he spoke as if he were their overworked servant. "Yes," he said wearily, "caring for them requires a lot of my time."

I moved quickly – while trying not to appear in a hurry – to get away, off to Kahlenberg mountain. Then I dawdled en route, eating some fruit and crackers in the Strauss-Lanner Park. My idea was to delay the climb down from the top of the mountain as long as possible so I could make it in the late afternoon light. I smiled at this sign of my leisured status, that I could not only spend the day making such an excursion, but even had the luxury of choosing the exact time period for it. By the way, the street bordering this park was one of the places where I spotted a poster for that magnum opus, *Gustav Klimt: das Musical.*

In the evening, Stefan was a little livelier. He wanted to talk about screwball comedies, and it turned out he'd probably seen more of them than I had. His knowledge came with a taint, that it was clearly gathered thanks to long hours spent alone in his apartment. He sat eternally at his kitchen table, fiddling around on his laptop. He didn't have WiFi, and to connect to the internet, I had to borrow his cable. This plainly caused him anxiety. After ten minutes, he asked, "Do you need the cable much longer?" I was partway through a response to an email from my ex, who wanted to know why, if I was traveling "all the time," he should continue to let me have custody of the boxed set of complete Mozart string quintets I'd received as part of our divorce settlement. "Have you got something to do that requires the internet?" I asked Stefan, struggling with the wording of my email, wanting to strike the right balance between understanding and assertiveness. "No," he admitted. I sensed he liked being hooked up to it constantly, like a child at his mother's breast.

I asked Stefan if he'd ever visited India. "No," he said, "but I did spend a month in Nepal. That was the most wonderful experience in my life." Difficult to believe when I learned he'd been sick for three of the four weeks, diarrhea coming and going. "I think what started the illness was seeing the body of a dead woman burned on a pyre. One of her legs fell off, and a worker got hold of it with a pitchfork and tossed it back on the pyre."

I had to think about this for a moment. "You're saying your illness might have started because of your mental reaction to seeing that, not from something physical?"

"Yes, perhaps," he said in his feeble voice.

The next morning, Stefan was back to his quieter self, like a wound-down toy. Over breakfast, I asked what kind of work he did. "I'm a craniosacral therapist," he said. "But I don't have enough clients now." Enough for what, he didn't explain. I'd spotted a folding massage table in my bedroom. I could imagine potential clients doubting they would received health at the hands of someone who seemed so unhealthy himself. Stefan was always slumped forward. When he gestured, his hands fell at the wrist, as if he didn't have the strength to maintain their connection with his arms.

When Stefan couldn't find something or remember something, he became disturbed. Talking about the Western powers flying supplies into West Berlin when the East blocked land access, he couldn't think of the English word "airlift." His hands fluttered, his eyes darted. I rushed in to end his agitation, exclaiming "Airlift, airlift!"

I asked Stefan if he visited his family. "As seldom as possible," he said. His father drank, his mother "produced many illnesses." Although his mother's sister lived in the house next door, with a common wall, she hadn't spoken to his mother in thirty years. "They had an argument, though I can't even remember what it was about. If my parents make too much noise, the sister calls the police."

I spent the day visiting Schloss Schönbrunn. Since I hadn't managed to coax Stefan out of the apartment for a meal, I brought him a bouquet of yellow roses and a bottle of wine from Napa. Giving him wine from my place of origin might have seemed a considered choice, when in fact it just occurred to me while hastily scanning the selection at a supermarket.

In the morning, I was late leaving Stefan's to reach the train station, my lack of punctuality rearing its ugly head. Although I did arrive in time, if anything had gone wrong on the way, I might have missed my train. Seated in a compartment, I covered a sheet of paper with sentences like, "I will leave on time. I'll leave when planned. I'll leave so that I'm not late. I will not be late. I *promise!*"

GERALD

Visiting the small, sleepy Austrian berg of Klagenfurt wasn't exactly a life-long dream of mine. However, I wanted to break up the long trip between Vienna and Udine. I chose Klagenfurt for this purpose because I'd found a gay host there – and from the photographs in his Couchsurfing profile, he looked kind of cute.

When Gerald opened the door of his apartment, I found he looked exactly like his photographs in his profile. These were neither out of date nor misleading, unlike most of the ones I found on dating websites. There was something odd, however, that he wore dark glasses. Come to think of it, he'd worn these same glasses in all his pictures. The small oval lenses weren't so dark that I couldn't see through them. What I saw also came as a surprise, that one of his eyes was open and the other, the left, shut. In addition, Gerald had a red circular scar at the base of his throat, in the exact center. I'd also noticed the scar in some of the photos and wondered what it was.

Gerald spoke to me slowly and apologized for his poor English. Of course, I thought, you speak a language you aren't fluent in more slowly. Soon I realized the slowness had another source. His facial muscles had to make some slight, continuous effort to produce the sounds, which came out a little blurred. "Illness," I said to myself, perhaps some sort of birth defect.

As we sat at his kitchen table sipping mugs of tea, Gerald apologized again, in this case for the weather, which was cool and drizzly. I said I'd had such good luck with the weather during most of my trip, I couldn't complain. . . . I settled down with the real Gerald, putting aside the one I'd vaguely imagined and lusted after based on his profile. His English still came out slow and blurred, but otherwise improved as the talk went on. He used some words and phrases that showed a fairly advanced level.

I was curious to know how Gerald had ended up in a small town like Klagenfurt. "Does your family live here?" I asked. "No, they live in Graz," he said. "That's two hours away by train." Instead, it was apparently a job that explained his presence.

He told me he'd found work in the local public library, and I assumed library jobs were as scarce in Austria as in the U.S.

I offered to take Gerald out to dinner. On our way to the center of town, I found he had a slightly lurching walk. I suggested we cut through a park, then was sorry, for he had some trouble maneuvering around the muddy patches. He gave the impression he couldn't always place his feet exactly where he wished. Instead, they landed more with a sense of approximation. To help him skirt one patch, I offered him my hand. It felt cold in mine.

"How did you find out about Couchsurfing?" I asked.

"I read an article on the internet and liked the idea. I've had ninety-seven guests," Gerald told me proudly.

"I didn't realize you'd had that many," I said.

"Lately, I've become more selective about which guests I accept. I only host people who are over twenty-five, and only single people because my apartment is so small. I have to go to work in the morning. What if first one guest, then another wanted to use the bathroom?"

Gerald was planning a trip to Switzerland in the summer. "I'll stay with two people I hosted, a man from Zurich and a woman from Lucerne."

"Those are great destinations," I said. "Lucerne is one of the most beautiful places I've ever seen. – Oh, look at the birds!" I pointed at a flock of them high in the sky.

Gerald said nothing at first. I didn't look over at him. Maybe he was peering up at the sky. "They're coming closer," he said at last. "It's like the Hitchcock movie," he joked.

I'd pointed out a couple of other things earlier, a mountain in the distance, a church. I told myself to stop doing this. I wasn't clear how well he saw anything. I wondered what he would see in beautiful Lucerne.

So often people said categorically that they were or weren't attracted to another person, as if this were always so cut and dried, either/or. For myself, attraction was more often a column of figures I had difficulty adding up. The sum came out this way one moment, another way the next. I was still working on the calculation with Gerald. All right, there were the obvious small physical defects. On the other hand, he was fifteen years younger than I was – and he had black hair, which was one of my fetishes. It was just the kind I liked, thick and glossy and contrasting with very white skin.

We were talking about the Austrians. "I hadn't realized before coming here that there are the fair Austrians and the dark Austrians," I said. "You're one of the dark ones." I couldn't resist placing my hand briefly on Gerald's beautiful black hair. This triggered something I couldn't have articulated even an instant later. The only thing I knew for sure was that we both stopped talking for a moment. Our contact gave me a black-hair thrill and I suspect touched some nerve in Gerald as well – though which? The nerve of excitement or the sad one of, "Hardly anyone ever touches me because I'm damaged goods"? Not mutually exclusive, of course.

While Klagenfurt was hardly a teaming metropolis, in the center we did encounter a fair number of people out strolling and shopping. One street intersected another at a sharp angle. As we passed around the angle, Gerald bumped into first one person, then another. Crossing a street, I took his arm, deciding it would be better if I guided him. I wasn't sure how he felt about this, though he didn't withdraw his arm.

To study the menu in the restaurant, Gerald removed his dark glasses and put on another pair, which were the same except the lenses were clear.

"You have two glasses," I said.

"Yes," he said. "These are for reading, the others for seeing farther away."

"My glasses are bifocals, so they work for both."

"I can only see straight ahead," Gerald said in his slow voice. "I can't turn my eyes down."

I paused. I didn't want to pry, yet he was bringing up the subject himself. "Can you see out of your other eye?"

"Yes." Reaching under the lens, Gerald lifted it with a finger. "The problem is the lid."

I'd never heard of that before, an eyelid not functioning. The eye could see, but the lid wouldn't raise and lower, rendering it useless.

"Did you have an accident?" I asked.

"Yes, in a car."

"How old were you?"

"Twenty. I had an operation on the eyelid. It worked for a few years. Then it stopped again." I didn't ask if he could have a second operation. I assumed not. "My other eye has learned to compensate," he said.

Arriving, I'd sat beside Gerald on the upholstered banquette. This had looked more comfortable than the wooden chair on the other side of the table, and sitting beside him seemed friendlier. From this angle, I could see his open eye. It looked slightly red. I thought how much it must be taxed, performing the work of two.

It was easy for me to imagine someone getting killed in a car accident. Plenty of movies and television shows had prepared me for this idea. Or the person was injured (a scene in a hospital room) and recovered (a scene with the person's arm or leg in a cast). I had no precedents for imagining what it would be like to have an accident and survive, yet have these smaller disabilities for the rest of your life. The eyelid that didn't function, the scar on the throat (from what, a stent?), some sort of effect on his speech, all making me conjecture the impact of the car crash had been mainly to his head. Some problem with coordinating the movements of his legs. Or was his faulty vision to blame for that?

Gerald talked about his job as a reference librarian. "I'm always learning something," he said. "I like helping people, answering their questions." I wondered how he felt when he considered how much his work involved seeing: reading printed pages, computer screens? I imagined his family wishing he lived nearer so they could help him more, and Gerald resisting, wanting to be independent.

I pondered how Couchsurfing fit into the picture. Did Gerald's desire to host so much have something to do with his physical condition? A stranger might be put off by it and slip away. A surfer staying in his home couldn't do that as easily. Still, after spending some time with Gerald, the surfer would see that he wasn't mentally defective, which his way of speaking suggested as a possibility. When Gerald ordered for us, his German came out rather slow and labored like his English.

"Have you met any of the other local Couchsurfing hosts?" I asked.

"Yes," he said. "We sometimes have functions." He added, smiling, "I hate all of them."

Why on earth would he hate them? I didn't ask. I was leaving for Udine tomorrow and taking only a sip from this man's life. I stayed at the smiling level. "Well, of course you're the best host in Klagenfurt," I said, as if this explained a mutual animosity. "You're the star."

It was dark by the time we walked back to the apartment. Gerald admitted he didn't see as well in the dark, and I kept hold of his arm the whole time. He didn't resist, nor did he definitely link his arm in mine, just letting it hang at his side.

Tucked up on Gerald's couch in his living room, I thought about something I never had before. The way my eyelids opened and closed, opened and closed.

LORENZO

Riding a south-bound bus the next day, I didn't notice when it crossed the border. There wasn't much to draw attention to borders in Europe nowadays, with unrestricted travel among EU countries. The first thing that alerted me to our arrival in Italy was a sign above the highway telling drivers to slow down: "*Ralentare.*" Out of the mountains and onto a plain. Arriving in Udine, I walked to the home of my first Italian host, Lorenzo, through a wind that was strong enough to blow off my hat.

Lorenzo was a mid-thirties Sicilian, balding, somewhat out of shape, though still with the appeal of the Italian for me. I loved the thick accent with which he spoke English, with vowels pronounced that we don't, turning "some" into a two syllable word. He added vowels that weren't even there in the written form. "Bit" was "bit-uh."

Although qualified to teach economics at the university level, at present Lorenzo was teaching math and science in a primary school. Still, he told me he enjoyed the work. He'd lived in Udine for seven years and was happy here, though he missed the warmer weather of Sicily. "In Sicily, I used to go to the beach every day. My mother called me yesterday and told me she'd just returned from the beach. That made me a little sad," pressing one hand to his heart. "Up here in the north, summer still hasn't arrived yet."

Dreary apartment with odds and ends of furniture that all belonged to Lorenzo's landlady. On the white walls, only a few small pictures, which were also hers. At thirty-five, Lorenzo owned little more than his books and clothes, though he did have a car.

Lorenzo wanted to go to the library to read the newspaper. He also went there to use the internet. "I don't want it in my home," he said. "I'd be afraid of getting addicted." The walk to the library took us farther into the center of town. The buildings became older (Lorenzo couldn't tell me how old, since as he said, he wasn't that interested in art and architecture), the street scene livelier. "Is this the *passeggiata*?" I asked. "Yes," Lorenzo said. After the muted public life of Austria, the streets crowded with strolling Italians came as a delight. There were couples, families, people walking dogs, old people who were by themselves, yet seeming to get something from taking part. Many people were dressed up, though an element of the crowd, mainly male, wore casual American clothes, shorts with pockets on the legs, T-shirts.

On Piazza Matteotti, a girl turned cartwheels, a boy rode his scooter, a girl wanted to pet the dog of a woman sitting on the steps before the fountain. Emphasizing that it was a stage, the main part of the piazza was raised several feet and free of accoutrements except for some light posts, the fountain, and a stone column topped by a Madonna and child. In Piazza Libertà stood a smaller cousin of the Doge's Palace in Venice, with a white and pink upper story resting on a loggia. People crossed the loggia or lingered there, looking over the balustrade. I admired the theatricality of the Italian cityscape, with the piazza a stage, the loggia a viewing platform.

I met Lorenzo in front of the library. "I go to this bakery that offers bread for half price in the last half hour before it closes," he said. "Lots of people come for the half price bread, but I managed to get one of the last loaves." He brandished his prize in a paper bag.

Lorenzo drove us to the apartment of Simone, an English teacher. A Russian friend of Simone's, Dasha, was visiting him, and we all set off in search of dinner. Dasha was a pretty, dark-haired woman, easy to talk to. Simone had met her while teaching Italian in Saint Petersburg, where she lived. The guys, sitting in front, changed their mind several times about where we should eat. We ended up traveling a long way out of town, making me joke to Dasha that they were kidnapping us.

Our destination was an *agriturismo*. We turned off the road onto a long dirt drive with a cornfield on one side. Ancient farm buildings were grouped around a rectangular space. One contained a restaurant. An open fireplace in a corner was surrounded by benches. The chimney reached down from the ceiling without touching anything below it. As I remarked to the others, most of the guests looked at us as we entered. Didn't "stare," only looked, as Europeans do – and to judge from this instance, Italians do in particular. They just seemed interested in seeing who we were.

No printed menu. The thin young waiter with a big upper lip, a son of the owners, had to tell us what was available. Later, it occurred to me he hadn't told us the price of anything, though the meal turned out to be quite cheap. The Italians translated for Dasha and me. We both got confused about which items were *primi piatti* and which *secondi*, though perhaps it didn't matter. Simone was patient about having to repeat himself, showing his teacher side.

My minestrone soup was delicious. I could declare in all sincerity that Italian food was the best in the world. "The French think they make the best food, but they don't."

Simone said, "French food is supposed to be more varied."

I disagreed and gave a comic description of a typical French meal. "It's always the same, a piece of meat with a delicious sauce accompanied by three tiny tiny carrots."

Secondo for me was fried soft cheese with polenta. Polenta was a feature of the local cuisine, which it wasn't in the south, as Lorenzo explained. Dasha was surprised that I ordered panna cota after not eating all of my second course. "This is my first day in Italy in a long time," I explained, "so I must have an Italian dessert."

Lorenzo and Simone, sitting across from me, looked something like brothers. They were about the same age, both losing their hair in the same way, both wearing similar black-framed glasses. Lorenzo was coarser looking, and tanned. He said he had a sore throat and kept clearing it. I resisted the temptation to make endless jokes about his not liking the cooler weather in the north.

I felt happy, a little more thanks to the place and being in Italy than my companions, who were strangers after all, despite our best intentions toward each other. Conversation patchy at times. At one point Lorenzo said, "It shows we are enjoying our food because no one is talking."

A man approached our table. I caught the word *macchina*. After the man had moved away, Lorenzo explained that several cars were blocking the man's car. The man went from table to table. The whole process took a long time, in a voluble Italian way. It started to rain beyond the open door, yet this just became part of the pleasant atmosphere of the place.

The next morning, Lorenzo told me he would study today. Simone and Dasha were going to Slovenia so Dasha could paraglide. Simone had offered to drop me in Cividale del Friuli, to the east of Udine, on the way. "You'll want to paraglide, too," I teased Simone, "once you see Dasha sailing through the air."

"No," he chuckled, "I'll stay on the ground and read." Camus, as I saw.

On the way to Cividale, we observed an altercation between two drivers. We could see the one behind gesturing, exclaiming something, which couldn't be heard by anyone else; not by the other driver nor, since the man was alone, by a companion. The man rolled down his window and splashed water from a bottle onto the rear windshield of the other car. While this sort of thing was diverting to watch, I wouldn't want that much anger directed at me.

Arriving in Cividale, though I'd been enjoying my companions, my loner side was glad not to have to talk with anyone for a while. I bought a four euro plate of polenta and *patatine fritte* from an *osteria* with an opening on the street. The man spoke to me in German, at least getting that I wasn't Italian. I ate sitting on a stool, resting my plate on a wooden shelf provided in the narrow street. Although the meal was small, I saved part and stored it in my shoulder bag. I liked stretching out my food consumption this way. Later in the day, I found the cheese cubes, which I'd forgotten I'd put in a separate plastic bag, and promptly ate them.

Near the main square, I passed a group of teenage girls dressed in folkloric costumes as part of some festival. My eyes rested on a couple of black girls, and one of them returned my gaze. Getting the attention of her companions, she gave an exaggerated, flouncy imitation of my walk. I could extrapolate that, feeling out of place in Italy, she needed to emphasize the ridiculousness of someone else. Still, I imagined marching over to her and exclaiming in my bad Italian that that wasn't a nice thing to do: "*Non è una cosa gentile da fare, signorina.*"

While I made an effort to normalize my walk, I gave up almost at once, sensing it was hopeless.

CLAUDIO

When I went to buy a ticket to Trieste at the train station in Udine, the machine instructed me using the voice of a woman with a thick Italian accent: "Insert-uh your card-uh."

Claudio, my Trieste host, met me at the station. Claudio was gay, and in his profile, he mentioned the possibility of guests sleeping in his bed. An immediate No to this idea from me on seeing him in person. He was pudgy and had a colorless mole beside his nose. Claudio's apartment contained a big flat-screen television; a multi-volumed Italian encyclopedia that, judging from the many knickknacks placed in front of it, was never touched; and a large cage containing two gray parrots with red tail feathers. Shades of Constance! While I was questioning Claudio about the birds, one pooped in the food plate at the bottom of the cage. As with Niklas and Milena's parrots, one bird was dominant. Claudio told me that Figaro, the alpha parrot, would fly around the room and sit on his shoulder, whereas the other refused to venture forth.

Claudio was on his midday break from his job at a supermarket. He made pasta for lunch, giving me a choice of which type I wanted. Figaro plucked at a screen at the bottom of the cage, producing quite a loud bang. "He wants some pasta, too," Claudio explained. He fed each of the birds a few strands.

Claudio's English not as good as Lorenzo's, which made me try some of my very limited Italian, a word or phrase here and there. This made me laugh, because I kept mixing up Italian and Spanish, which my brain couldn't keep in separate compartments.

Claudio had a boyfriend, Manuel. They'd met when Claudio was thirty-two and supervising a church youth group that included Manuel, who was fourteen at the time. After the group disbanded at the end of summer, Manuel approached Claudio and said he wanted to be friends. Their relationship wasn't sexual at first. Claudio gave an extremely long, detailed description of Manuel's family problems. These included an alcoholic wife-beating father who finally killed himself, using the same method his mother had of slitting his wrists in a bathtub. The story was made especially long by Claudio's frequent hesitations over his English. Claudio referred to Manuel as "my angel," which I thought was touching.

On his way back to work, Claudio dropped me in the Piazza Dell'Unità d'Italia, the main architectural showpiece of the city. Peering skeptically at the elegant, yet frigid buildings surrounding me on three sides, I thought, "I'm sure I won't like Trieste." From what I'd seen of other parts of the city, it reminded me of Genoa, Italy scruffy and down-at-heels.

I went through the tourist motions, though I spent a large part of the afternoon sitting in a pew in Trieste Cathedral reading *Of Human Bondage*. Thank God, I found this novel engrossing. I couldn't help seeing the deformity of the main character's club foot as a stand-in for the author's deformity of homosexuality. Leaving the church, I was aware of my own feet, as if I'd assumed the character's identity.

Back at the apartment, I met Manuel. Claudio told me Manuel was tired from his job; I forget what kind of work he did. Manuel said little, then disappeared into the bedroom. On a trip to the bathroom, I glimpsed him sitting on the edge of the bed consulting his mobile, that great twenty-first century pastime.

For dinner, Claudio made another pasta dish, with me contributing fruit and cookies. Annalisa, a friend he nicknamed *la tigre*, as in "man-eater," dropped by. Earlier, Claudio had told me another long story, this one about Annalisa's involvement with a man in Croatia who was also seeing another woman. I couldn't follow this very well. Annalisa had long brown hair, small eyes, and wore denim shorts so abbreviated they were almost the size of swimming trunks. I was unclear why she'd been invited over. Not for my sake, I assumed, since her English was minimal. She was constantly asking Claudio words and phrases in English. Given the limitations of his own English, this was comical.

All the while, the television was on, tuned to a talent show involving a gaggle of model-thin young women. I tried to ask Annalisa if she liked this show, if it bothered her to see women treated as sex objects. However, I couldn't cross the language barrier. Claudio didn't really understand my questions either. All he could say was, "Both men and women watch this show."

After Annalisa left, Claudio got out a picture book about Trieste and went through it with me page by page. "Here's the Greek Orthodox Church. . . . This is the Serbian Orthodox church. . . . And that's the synagogue, one of the biggest in Europe. Many different types of people live in Trieste, but everyone gets along," Claudio assured me. I was happy to have this soothing narrative go on and on, like a child being read to.

The following day, Claudio came home at two o'clock for his long mid-day break. He'd been working in the fish section of the supermarket and took a shower to remove the smell. Over lunch, he talked about his job. "With some customers, if I offer them one piece of fish, they want another. They're suspicious I'm trying to get rid of it. With people like that, I offer them a good piece of fish and let them select a bad one instead."

Yesterday, I'd told Claudio I was tired and wanted to rest today. He'd suggested I spend the morning in the apartment, then in the afternoon go to Miramare Castle. I didn't intend to go out at all, but had waited until now to say I thought I would stay in during the afternoon as well. I wrote in my journal and dealt with some business matters. The parrots made various whistling sounds from their cage or rang the bell that hung from the upper bar. Noise-phobic, I would never dream of adding noise-making birds to my life, yet my annoyance with them was mixed with amusement. To the tune of "*La donna è mobile*," I sang to them, "I'm-uh gonna strangle you! That is what I'm-uh gonna do!"

In the evening, first Manuel, then Claudio returned. They were joined by their friend Giacomo, a wisp of a man, his extreme smallness and thinness accentuated by a stoop. After stays with lone Austrian wolves in Vienna and Klagenfurt, it was interesting to have these larger casts of characters with both my Italian hosts. Like Claudio, Giacomo had been born in Trieste. His English was minimal. He asked if he could turn on the news. I agreed, thinking, "Yes, it's simpler for us to watch television than struggle to communicate." I suggested he sit down. "No," he said, "I am a postman and I walk all day. I prefer to stand." I would have thought that after walking a lot, he would rather sit. I said, "I love to sit. I can sit all day long," a fact I'd proved earlier.

Claudio made dinner for Giacomo and me. Claudio himself had eaten at the house of his mother, whom he visited every day, and Manuel must have already had his dinner elsewhere. I turned off the television when we sat down to eat. Giacomo turned it back on, to another all-women talent show. Their talents included playing a child's game with string and one drawing a picture on another's back. At one point in the show, they danced together in a rudimentary way enforced by absurdly high heels.

Claudio had a maternal, or at least parental, quality. I imagined I saw his mother in his cooking for me and others. His attitude toward Manuel certainly had something of the parent in it. While I couldn't understand most of what the two men said to each other, their stances seemed clear enough. I got that Manuel didn't want to join us on a *passeggiata* because he had to write to his sister regarding their father's house, which they'd inherited. Claudio insisted he come, though he did this quietly.

The four us drove to the Piazza Dell'Unità d'Italia. The buildings on the square were beautifully lit at night. I thought it sad that Trieste (so close to *triste*, sad, as I was sure I wasn't the first person to remark) had this one impressive, but unlovable square to offer visitors, and not much else. We ate gelato from a gelateria that Claudio said was the best in the city. While I'm not a big fan of gelato, my chocolate and cherry "mon chéri" was truly remarkable, even including some undertones, like a fine wine. It melted very fast, making me lick quickly. I wondered if the speedy melting was one sign of its high quality.

Our interactions were fragmented as we wandered about. Manuel kept looking at his mobile. Claudio appeared distracted much of the time, perhaps in part by Manuel's own lack of focus. Giacomo didn't say much, though he smiled agreeably, looking out from behind his owlish spectacles (Claudio described Giacomo to me as a "simple man," which seemed apt). I didn't particularly care. I enjoyed the bits of talk as they came, the taste of the gelato, the balmy wind blowing from the sea. Claudio and I didn't have much in common, yet I couldn't help liking him, he was so kind and hospitable. Taking my cue from Giacomo, I just smiled a lot.

We returned to the piazza, which at this late hour contained mostly university students, bunched at the end farthest from the sea and the wind. In a group near us, three young Englishmen introduced themselves to three young Italian women. One man shook hands with them in turn, then repeated the process, saying their names again to make sure he had them right. Another kissed the girls on the cheek instead. All of them were smiling, laughing. I said to Claudio as the group moved away, "They'll marry each other, and have children, and remember this night for the rest of their lives because it was when they met."

As the end of the chapter approaches, let's return to *Do I Hear a Waltz?* This musical should be famous, or notorious, for no other reason than that it ranks high among cats-in-a-sack collaborative artistic works. Stephen Sondheim called it a "poison pill," offering him a chance to pay his dues to his mentor Oscar Hammerstein by collaborating with Richard Rodgers after Hammerstein died. Rodgers dismissed Sondheim's lyrics as "shit" in front of the cast. Arthur Laurents, who wrote the book, believed his own choice of John Dexter as director proved a "deadly error." Herbert Ross, the choreographer, later said the leading lady, Elizabeth Allen, was miscast, "too young, not vulnerable enough." Wakefield Poole, the choreographic assistant (who later gained fame as a gay porn pioneer), criticized Sergio Franchi, the male lead, as "sterile." Laurents: "The show had no style, no concept." Sondheim: "It deserved to fail." For me, it's a fascinating crossroads work, with Rodgers' music sounding like early Sondheim and Sondheim's lyrics resembling late Hammerstein.

Not surprisingly, this musical reviled even by those who brought it into being was never made into a movie. I haven't

seen it performed on stage, and I know it only from the cast recording and the piano score. For a visual component, I turn to
Summertime, a film David Lean made ten years earlier based on
the same story, with Katherine Hepburn in the lead. The musical and the film merge for me, though not quite to the extent
of my imagining Hepburn belting out the opening number in
the middle of Piazza San Marco.

At the end of the film, Rossano Brazzi just misses seeing
Hepburn off at the train station, though if an audience member
can summon up some objectivity in the midst of all the cine-
matic razzle dazzle, he'll realize that in fact Brazzi had ample
time to get there. Hepburn waves at him from the window of
her train as it races along the causeway toward the mainland.
After bidding goodbye to Claudio and Trieste, I rode the train
in the other direction, from the mainland toward Venice. Sea
and sky were like a blank page, the sea featureless and the sky
almost so, with something very thin and darkish in between.
Gradually the thin darkish something grew more distinct,
transforming into the water-borne city.

I'd visited Venice twice with my ex. Feeling I'd had my fill
of this dish, I was only coming here again because I was flying
out of Marco Polo Airport in a couple of days. I didn't even
have any surfing adventures to look forward to. I hadn't bothered to search for a host here, assuming it was nearly impos-
sible to find one. Instead, I was staying at a hostel, though at
least I'd found one without bunk beds. I hadn't hurried to get
here from Trieste, taking a train in the early afternoon. Once
I emerged from the station and took in the scene, the Grand
Canal with its bustling water traffic, the odd narrow church
on the opposite side, I was more excited to be in Venice than
I'd expected. At the hostel, my emotion showed in my asking
the Polish receptionist, "How long has the hostel been here?"

It took the woman a while to grasp my question, and maybe also to understand why in the world I cared. "Eight years," she said at last.

The hostel was near Piazzale Roma and the park where I'd met Giulio forty years ago. I made a pilgrimage there. The park looked smaller than I remembered. A couple of food stands had been added. At one, a man asked a customer if he wanted cheese on his sandwich. The row of benches where Giulio and I had sat for our first conversation had been removed, so that people had to perch on the rough stones edging the planted sections. A man spat.

To have some time with my memories, I retreated to the larger park on the other side of a minor canal. There, I said hello to Giulio in my mind, speaking to him across time and possibly the life-death boundary, since he might very well be dead by now. "I remember you, and I'm grateful," I told him. When Giulio spoke to me on that night long ago, could he have imagined I would write a story about him one day, that I would be sitting here many years later thinking about him?

I set out along the minor canal. The city was in full tourist spate, people crowding the pavements. As I moved along, my mind sometimes turned to Giulio again. "All right," I said to myself, "you had your quarter hour of paying tribute to this memory. Don't use wallowing in the past to distract yourself from the here and now. Maybe you can have some *new* adventures." I paused on one of the many bridges and watched a motorboat glide away from me down the long, straight canal. It grew ever smaller, and I tried to make my memory do the same, until at last it was just a minor dot in the larger view.

Chapter 7

United Kingdom and Ireland: The King and I

CAMERON

In the event, my time in Venice was short on adventures. It wasn't one of the romantic numbers from *Waltz?* that kept recurring, rather "Here We are Again." In this song, the heroine sits by herself in a Venetian cafe, trying not to mind being alone among all the bustling groups and couples. The "we" in question consists of the heroine and herself, and lacking anyone else to talk with, she carries on a wistful inner dialogue.

Musicals had a gift for encapsulating particular situations and their emotional stances. I was grateful to *Waltz?* for capturing this one, especially since it was much less common in musicals, if not in life, than the situation of someone bursting at the seams with love, love, love. I felt less alone to imagine the heroine in similar circumstances, with the composer, lyricist, and director near at hand, and beyond them, a sympathetic audience.

Arriving at Heathrow, I was happy that the people around me spoke English for a change. I enjoyed the various British accents, which I thought of as "cute." In the display panel in the train, a message came on saying that if one didn't have a first-class ticket, one should vacate the first-class area. I was reminded of the hyper-instructiveness of the British, in this case communicating something that seemed self-evident.

The politeness of the British was on show as I made my way to Cameron, my host, in Lambeth. Overhearing me question the bus driver, another passenger told me where to get off. A bicyclist I asked for directions found the address I was looking for on the map on his mobile. He actually apologizing for taking so long.

Before starting my search for a host in London, I'd heard from other surfers that this was among the most difficult places to find one, followed closely by other hyper popular destinations like New York. Thinking of myself as a seasoned campaigner by this time, I refined my techniques. Confronted with profile after profile, I ran my eye down the middle of the text, hoping to pick up enough of the information on either side to let me make a quick evaluation. I learned that with male hosts, the first thing to look at was their references. Specifically, the names of the people leaving them. If all the references were from women – Stella, Vanessa, Lorena, Larissa – I could infer the man was using Couchsurfing as a dating service and would almost certainly not host me.

Deciding that I, too, could play the game of specialization, I searched for "gay" in the London profiles. Cameron's among the ones this turned up. Although Cameron apparently wasn't gay himself, he'd used the word when filling in "Types of

People I Enjoy." "Enjoy? Those who treat others as they wish to be treated. All, whether atheist, Muslim, Buddhist, young, old, gay, straight, black, white, tall, short, chubby, slim, rich, poor. All are equal in the eyes of God."

Cameron was a Christian as it turned out, living in an all-male household with other members of his church. He accepted only male guests, presumably to avoid any risk of carnal temptation, and asked that in exchange for his hospitality, they attend a service with him. Although making a condition of this kind was against the Couchsurfing philosophy, with no one else agreeing to host, I accepted. Staying with Cameron did at least offer "weird value."

Cameron had said he would leave a key for me in the recycling bin if I arrived after eleven at night. It was after midnight by the time I came through the door, but there he was, still awake. He was a vaguely attractive middle-aged man with wide open eyes that had a quality of blankness or innocence, I couldn't determine which.

Since three other guests were occupying the living room, I slept on a narrow mattress in Cameron's study. By the time I was up and showered, Cameron had returned from taking some Canadian surfers to Heathrow and collecting two Portuguese ones. These were Nuno and Miguel, medical students visiting London for a week.

Over a breakfast of porridge, in a spirit of diving in, I asked Ross, one of the other "serious Christians" living in the house, why the crucifixion was so important. This had puzzled me, confronted by countless gruesome bodies nailed to crosses in the European churches I'd visited. "The crucifixion shows God assuming human form and sharing in our suffering, instead of standing apart from it," he said. "If we see God suffering, we can expect him to understand our own suffering."

During our talk on this subject, the Portuguese didn't say a word, concentrating on their porridge. To take part in a theological discussion probably wasn't one of their reasons for coming to London.

Cameron whisked Nuno and Miguel off to visit Greenwich. He had a curious obsession with Greenwich. I must have heard him recommend it as a day trip four or five times during my visit. I mused whether Greenwich had some hidden Christian significance à la Dan Brown, if taking people there was somehow part of Cameron's plan to win converts.

Declining an invitation to join the party, I set off for the city center. Walking through the Victoria Embankment Gardens, I was glad to be back in London. Wasn't this often my feeling upon arriving here, of being back somewhere that was, if not exactly home, at least after many visits fairly home-like? The cool, gray, drizzly weather a refreshing contrast to mainly sunny Italy, though I knew I'd probably tire of it in a day or two.

Happening on a cafe in the Gardens, with the effects of a small bowl of porridge wearing off, I ate a full English breakfast sitting outside under an umbrella. I relished everything I saw – the huge old plane trees with bumpy tan bark, a couple of commemorative statues, one including a small camel – and everything I ate, the tea with milk and sugar, the beans and sausages and ham slices.

I'm so much an Anglophile, other national philias didn't even present themselves as alternatives until I was well into adulthood. My family background is unadulterated WASP. I grew up reading mainly books by British authors. The BBC, as channeled through PBS, was my main provider of cultural enrichment and higher-toned entertainment (it took me a long time to realize how people could make fun of the top-lofty title, *Masterpiece Theatre*). My first trip outside North America was to the U.K. with my parents, when at fourteen I combined the impressionability of a child with the beginnings of a more adult point of view.

It might seem unlikely that musicals would play a part in this bent, yet they do. My family only had a small number of records when I was growing up. Five of these were musicals. I'm sure of the exact number because I clearly remember each of the five, the songs, even the record jackets. *The King and I*, from the movie version, was a particular favorite. On the back of the jacket, I underscored with a childish line the word "irate" in the telling of the story, a word I didn't know: "Anna, irate and disappointed, prepares to leave the palace." I drew hair on Yul Brynner's bald head. The earliest dream I can remember involved Yul Brynner turned into a giant who held Anna and me in the palm of his hand.

In a nice small-town tradition that I hope is continued, every year Napa would stage a musical. Once it was *The King and I*. As a child I was fascinated to see the walls of the King's palace open to reveal the garden where Tuptim and Lun Tha had their secret rendezvous. I longed to play the part of Anna's son, sure I could have done as good a job as the boy in this production. With Brit culture such an influential part of my childhood, it's fitting I would take to heart this tale of a plucky British lady bringing this same culture to benighted Siam.

That evening, I dutifully showed up for a service at Cameron's church. This possessed a grand columned facade that had survived Nazi bombing and a tepid Fifties replacement to the building proper, which had not.

Ross met me at the door. We sat in the balcony with a young woman who had the same sort of smile he did. Agreeable, though with something slightly pointed about it. A large congregation was assembled, a quarter black, with a wide age range. Cameron sat off to the left with the Portuguese men, each also paired with a woman. I later learned that one of these women, or possibly both, spoke Portuguese. The strategy was transparent, though I wanted to say to Cameron, "Couldn't you at least have hooked me up with some cute guy? Maybe then I'd convert."

The minister entered with hands folded in front of him and mounted the steps to the pulpit. He had a dry face that became rather unpleasant around the mouth. It was warm in the balcony. Tired after a day careening around London, I almost dozed off during the sermon. This took as its basis the rich man who had prompted the famous saying about the camel going through the eye of the needle. The theme was how demanding God was. "God wants more from us than good works and half-hearted allegiance. He demands unquestioning faith and complete submission to his will." Whatever that was imagined to be, I added privately. The young woman made notes, her printing so clear I could read some of it from where I sat.

In the vestibule afterward, Cameron asked what I'd thought of the service. I made some random remarks, omitting that it was the least appealing service of the admittedly few I'd attended in my life. I walked back to the house with Ross. He told me how he'd joined this church. "I tried out several others, but I didn't find them Bible-based enough. The ministers sounded more like therapists, trying to make people feel good about themselves, which isn't the point." The others must have returned faster by bus or car, for there they were seated around the kitchen table, eating leftovers from the food served at the church.

I moved down from Cameron's studio to the living room, sharing it with the Portuguese. As I was getting ready for bed, Fernando, the Colombian housemate, entered with an open

Bible. He asked me to read a few verses from First Corinthians, where Paul described the unrighteous who wouldn't inherit the Kingdom of God. The "effeminate" were among them, which gave me a big fat clue of what was coming, especially since I'd made a couple of allusions that evening to being gay. Fernando approached the subject in such a roundabout manner that I had to wait several minutes for the word "homosexual" to appear. There were degrees of sinfulness, and while homosexuality was a sin of a less serious degree than some others – at this point I stopped him. "I'm tired," I said. "Maybe we can discuss this in the morning." When he persisted, I said, "Talking about this is a waste of your time and mine. Neither of us is going to change the other's mind."

This got rid of Fernando, though it left me to debate during the night what I should say about the incident to Cameron. It was only in the first few minutes that I considered saying nothing. "Don't be spineless," I told myself. If Cameron did turn out to be homophobic, I needed to say this in a reference, as a warning to other surfers.

I spoke to Cameron just before I left in the morning, when I could be alone with him in his study. After telling him what had happened, I asked, "Are gay people accepted in your home as they are or as people who need to change?" While he didn't explicitly say he accepted them, he did apologize for Fernando, saying he could be "brutal." He said he wasn't responsible for the opinions of his housemates.

Cameron took the opportunity to ask again, in a tone of wistful hopefulness, if I'd been affected by the service last night. "Have you ever heard the Word preached in that way before? I hadn't, before coming to this church."

The best I could do was to say I'd found the service "interesting."

Earlier, Cameron had told me he would give me a copy of *The Pilgrim's Progress*. I could see a row of these on a shelf in the study. As we parted, he failed to take one down and present it to me, suggesting I'd proved a disappointment.

HOLLY

"Lovely," said the burly man selling me a ticket at Paddington Station when I told him I wanted to go to Oxford. I liked being in a country where burly men used words like "lovely." It was a sunny day, a rare treat in Jolly Old Gray England. I looked at the green fields out the train window, one like green fur.

Let's imagine me singing "I Whistle a Happy Tune" to buck me up as I made my way through the streets of Oxford to my next host. In truth, I don't believe I did sing or even whistle this song, yet *The King and I* is already such a melange of fact and fiction, it hardly matters if I add another dash of fantasy where it's concerned. Although claiming she came from Wales to account for her dark coloring, that supposedly quintessential Brit Anna Leonowens was actually born in India. According to a recent biographer, she probably had a grandmother who was at least part Indian. Maybe tawny Rita Moreno should have played her in the movie instead of lily white Deborah Kerr. While there was indeed a King Mongkut, he didn't die almost in Anna's arms, rather while she was dillydallying in England, overstaying a six months leave from the court. Yul Brynner, the quintessential King, was a Russian-American. None of the children in the original Broadway cast was Thai. "Etcetera, etcetera, etcetera," as the King would say.

Any trepidation I might have had about meeting my next host was quickly laid to rest. I felt instantly at ease with Holly, and it didn't hurt that she was young, slim, and pretty. The only flaw in her looks were some slightly crooked teeth; but then this was Britain, where people weren't so obsessed with dental work. Holly had a pleasant voice and an educated accent. Americans have a reputation among Europeans of asking personal questions. Taking advantage of my American status, I asked Holly if she'd grown up speaking this way. "Yes," she said, "though some of my childhood friends in Southampton spoke differently." She imitated their accent, which I would *not* have described as educated. It was inconceivable that I and my own childhood friends in the U.S. could have sounded so different.

As a child, Holly said, she'd understood it was important to her parents that she pass the exam to get into a special local academy. She'd succeeded, and looking back, she could see this was a crucial fork in the road for her. Since she lived in Oxford, I'd assumed Holly had attended one of the colleges here. "No," she said, "I didn't even apply. I didn't want to be a small fish in a big pond."

Holly was an archaeologist, working in a small local museum in a nearby town. Since this job didn't pay well, she also had a part-time job at a pub. This was where she'd met her boyfriend (this went onto my how-they-met list: "job at pub"). "He used to flirt with me while I was behind the bar," she said. "He's tall and good-looking, and for a long time, I thought he must just be a lad, chasing after lots of girls. I made him work hard to prove he wasn't."

Over dinner at a nearby restaurant, Holly told me how she'd become an archaeologist. "At university, I took a class in Museums because it didn't require exams, only essays. One essay I wrote was about visiting a cocaine museum in La Paz. I just tossed it off, yet my professor liked it so much, she arranged for me to take part in a dig in Egypt." This dig was another fork in the road, leading her to major in Archaeology and write a dissertation that discussed how museums in Egypt and ones in Europe displayed Egyptian artifacts differently.

"Have you ever visited Egypt?" Holly asked.

"No," I said. "Nothing I've ever heard about it has made me want to go there. The traffic in Cairo is supposed to be so bad, you almost can't cross the street. And people are trying to sell you things everywhere, which is one of my pet peeves."

"Once I got past things like that, I found that Egyptians are the friendliest people I've ever met." Holly said she was going back in November to work on another dig.

"November," I mused. I pondered whether my money would hold out that long. "Could I visit you there?"

"That would be lovely," she smiled. More "lovely" in the lovely land of England. "I'm sure I can find some old tomb for you to sleep in."

As practice for sleeping in unusual locales like a tomb, I spent the night on a mattress in Holly's attic, reached by a ladder let down into the upper hallway.

LISA AND CRAIG

Holly could only host me for one night since she had a friend coming to visit, and I moved on to another host for my other two nights in Oxford. This was a couple: Craig, an American teaching at Oxford Brookes University, and his wife Lisa, a German studying business at the same school. Craig's body spilled over his belt like a cartoon character's. Individual pale hairs stood straight up on his head. That he'd found a reasonably attractive woman to marry made me envy straight men. I rarely saw such disparity of looks in gay couples. Lisa had spent so much time in the U.S. as a child, she considered herself equally American, and she spoke English with only a faint German accent. We ate sandwiches, sitting in their back yard.

The couple had identified themselves on their profile as publishers. In our talk, I learned they were on the point of bringing out their first two books. One was a cookbook with recipes contributed by various musicians, the other a children's book by an eleven-year-old. When Lisa asked what my novel was about, I told her. I waited to see if they would ask to take a look at it. They didn't. Suddenly, that they were publishers vanished from the conversation. Perhaps my pitch wasn't as good as the eleven-year-old's.

Craig and Lisa walked me partway into the center of Oxford with their dog. This Czech wolfhound acted as a hearing aid dog for Craig, who was hard of hearing and wore a hearing aid in each ear. They'd named the dog Mozart, which I thought was pretentious. I won a brownie point by saying, when Lisa pointed out they'd given the name to a female dog, that maybe they were thinking of Constanze. Seeing they were pleased I knew the name of the wife of their favorite composer, I said, "I'm so annoyed every time I think of that silly woman, going off to spas all the time when it was really her husband who needed looking after."

Setting off on my own, I visited a string of colleges. The variation is one of my favorite musical forms, and I was fascinated by the variations on a theme the colleges presented: gateway, porter's lodge, dining halls, chapels, gardens. I objected to the signs in some colleges indicating the "tourist route." I'd rather have been referred to as a "visitor."

At seven I met up with Lisa, Craig, and Mozart at Oxford Brookes. We attended an end-of-term social gathering of international students. Listening to Craig talk to me about the English legal system, I had my moment of deciding I found him boring. It seemed in character that Craig was hard of hearing. I'd had a boss who was hard of hearing, and like Craig, he appeared to have lost sensitivity toward his audience, operating in his own world. While Craig could put words out, he had trouble taking them in. He was a teacher to boot, with the habit of lecturing.

Later, I talked with an Italian girl and a Czech girl. When I told them I was Couchsurfing, they said they'd never heard of this and were intrigued. I said that for me, Couchsurfing had picked up where four years of therapy left off, "and unlike therapy, Couchsurfing saves you money rather than costing a lot." It was helping me become less afraid of things, I said, more adaptable.

In the morning, Lisa made a hearty breakfast. As she set down a plate heaped with food before Craig, he lamented that he'd gained weight in the last two weeks. "You gained it, and you'll lose it again," she said reassuringly.

Passing a Baptist Church on the way home last night had led to me telling the couple about my encounter with the Bible-wielding Colombian in London. They'd hardly responded, and I asked myself if maybe they, too, were anti-gay. This morning, they seemed gay-friendly, mentioning gay friends of theirs.

"When I lived in San Francisco," Craig said, "I used to hang out in the Castro with Hector, a straight buddy of mine."

"Why would two straight guys hang out there?" I asked.

"Hector's mom was a lesbian," Craig said, as if this answered my question. "Guys on Castro Street would made wolf calls at me," he said. Given Craig's appearance, this struck me as unlikely, barring a precipitous fall from good looks.

I returned to the city center. A half-dozen people stood in front of the Sheldonian Theatre holding signs saying,

"Welcome to Oxford, City of Animal Abuse," and "Oxford University Tortures Animals." At the sound of a cyclist approaching from behind, I moved off a path, and he said in a cultured voice as he passed, "That's very kind." In a store, I overheard one worker say to another in a less cultured voice, "If I get peckish, I can eat me tongue sandwich."

In the evening, I took Lisa and Craig out to dinner. They told me the story of how they'd met. Craig's mother had almost sunk their budding relationship when she intercepted all their letters, both the incoming ones from Lisa and the outgoing ones of her son, leaving each to think the other wasn't responding. "We only found out about this many years later when I came across a box with the letters in her house," Lisa said. Putting her hand on my arm, "You have to put that in a story."

"That's an amazing thing to have happen in real life," I said, "but in a story, I think it would seem contrived."

"No, you *must* use it," she insisted, her tone suggesting she knew better.

Yesterday, I'd bought a half-dozen books at an Oxfam shop, which thanks to its location had the most esoteric collection of any charity shop or used book store I'd ever seen. Six books coming in encouraged me to part with a similar number I'd finished with (not necessarily finished, but finished with). After attaching post-its to the covers saying "Read me," I scattered these en route to the bus station, on benches, retaining walls, wherever a flat surface offered itself. Before this trip, I'd kept most books I bought to create that odious thing called a "collection." Travel had taught me the pleasure of releasing them back into the wild instead. Thoreau should have followed his famous admonishment, "Simplify, simplify" with "and travel, travel, will teach you how." You lose some things when you travel, no matter how careful you are; because your suitcase is too heavy or packed too tightly, you shed others; and you realize you probably didn't need any of this stuff as much as you'd supposed. On the bus ride to Edinburgh, I imagined with a sort of rapture all the things in my home I would give away or throw away once I returned to San Francisco.

RHYS

I had a long time to muse on this subject, for the ride to Edinburgh took all day, mostly on winding two-lane roads. As usual on a long-distance bus, I took off my shoes and curled one or two legs under me on the seat. Recently I'd gotten my wish that tight pants would come back into fashion. This meant that with my nylon long johns underneath to protect me from the British chill, my legs were pretty tightly encased. About halfway through the trip, revolting at the strain, my pants – my only pair – tore at the crotch. Fortunately the tear didn't show. At least I hoped it didn't.

I was surfing with Rhys, who lived south of the city center. Rhys showed me into a room that was the nicest I'd stayed in as a surfer. It even had a window seat with cushions and a view of Salisbury Crags. Rhys was good-looking, with round shiny blue eyes. His profile gave his age as forty-two. Later, he admitted he'd shaved off ten years.

Rhys had turned hosting into a real operation. He told me the complicated schedule of who was coming and going in the flat, which had four bedrooms and two bathrooms. He combined surfers with longer-term paying guests. He made a salmon dinner for me and another surfer, Akmal, a thin young Malaysian who spoke perfect American-sounding English. Akmal had come to Edinburgh to appear in a dance performance and ended up staying with Rhys for a week.

While we ate, Rhys talked about his work as a seismologist. This visitor from a city poised on the Ring of Fire couldn't help looking amused by the idea of a seismologist in Britain, a land not known for its tremblors. "Minor earthquakes do occur here," Rhys assured me, "and the local seismic activity needs to be monitored." A recent sonic boom produced by military aircraft was creating a surge of inquiries to his department, and he spent some time reviewing these on his computer.

In a generally free-form trip, I did have several fixed dates to work around. One was the opening of my play, *Gaydonia*. This had been selected in its annual competition by the Luvvies, a gay theater company in Edinburgh. I'd like to say *Gaydonia* won out over a slew of entries. In fact, there were only two others. I'd also like to claim my play was the company's first choice when in truth it chose another one initially, then dropped it after the two co-authors had a falling out.

Rhys and Akmal accompanied me to St. Bride's Centre, where the play was being performed. One of the Luvvies' conditions for staging the play was that I give it a free hand; and of course it wouldn't pay me anything. The free hand had included freedom from almost any communication with me, so that I had no idea what to expect. That St. Bride's was located far from the city center already whispered in my ear, "Amateur production."

I'd asked the Luvvies for two comp tickets, one for myself and another for Rhys. Rhys asked Heather, the producer, who was manning the ticket desk, for a third comp ticket for Akmal. Although she gave him one, she plainly wasn't happy about this. "You asked for *two* comps," she told me with a pinched expression.

St. Bride's was a converted church. Portable tiers of seats filled one end of the nave. The theater could accommodate two hundred and fifty people. We had an audience of closer to the fifty without the two hundred. I led my little party to seats in the front row in order to minimize my awareness of the discrepancy between audience size and theater size.

"Yes, there's the map!" I cried to myself as it was wheeled out for the first scene; the map showing the Balkans and the tiny imaginary country of Zablvacia – soon to be transformed into Gaydonia – where the story was set. I giggled, I was delighted. In the second scene, the members of the Matosic family were gathered together in their living room. Most of them spoke with some approximation of a Serbo-Croatian accent, which I hadn't expected amateurs to attempt. With his accent and shaved head, the actor playing Davor Matosic, the male lead, reminded me of a skinny Yul Brynner. Maybe *The King and I* was on my mind. Thankfully, he was pretty good. So was about half the cast. Then there was the other half.

As the play continued, the novelty of seeing my work performed wore off and I became more aware of the shortcomings in the production. My vision had been of the actors rushing on and off stage, scrambling in and out of funny wigs and costumes. Instead, they all *strolled* on, with no sense of urgency. I heard someone behind me yawn. The church-turned-theater was chilly, which probably didn't raise the enthusiasm level of the audience. I hadn't had time yet to buy a new pair of pants and fancied I could feel a Scottish wind whistling through the tear.

Although I hadn't achieved my ambition to write a musical, I did at least include a song in my one and possibly only play, sung by the grandmother at the Gaydonia Folkloric Evening. Alas, the woman cast as the grandmother insisted she was tone deaf, as I later learned, and the song was cut, as was the entire scene in which it appeared. Even with these trimmings, thanks to sluggish pacing or my overwriting or both, the play ran for a somewhat grueling two hours plus. That didn't even include a fifteen minute intermission, or "interval," as it was identified on my program in British-ese. Tepid applause at the end. Not enough of it to warrant a second curtain call after the first. Hugh, the director, addressed the audience. He announced that the author of the play was present, pointing me out. I stood up, raising my right hand in a sort of queenly salute, then promptly sat down. That was the best I could do.

Thank God for Couchsurfing! Otherwise, I would have been attending my opening night alone and walking away from it without anyone to talk with. When I'd sent Rhys my couch request, he'd written back that he'd read a notice about the play and wanted to see it. However, neither in his profile nor his conversation so far had he definitely come out to me. This happened only as we discussed the play on the way back to his place. He said he liked that it criticized gay conformism (which in fact it didn't particularly). I asked Akmal for "the Malaysian perspective" on the play.

The next day, I met Hugh at An-tea-ques, a combination antique shop and tea room. Sitting down on a pink-upholstered sofa, I said, "This is like having tea in an antiques shop. Which of course is exactly what we're doing!" Hugh told me the cast had had just one rehearsal in which everyone managed to turn up on the same evening. This went some way to explaining the deficiencies of opening night. The Luvvies had put on the show with a budget of a mere fifteen hundred pounds, most of the money used for renting the church-turned-theater.

That evening at the second performance, some lines that had been omitted in the first turned up mysteriously. Looking at the program, I found it contained a biography of everyone involved in the production except me, the author. No one had written to ask me for one.

Before the third and last performance on Sunday evening, Hugh told me people were going out for a drink after the show, once the set was struck. I hung around while the cast not only struck the set, but dismantled the theater seats, presumably so the Center could be used for other purposes. The cast slipped away by ones and twos. It looked like a rollicking drinks fest wasn't any more likely to materialize with this group than a rollicking performance. I removed a couple of posters for the play from the lobby as mementos and slipped away myself.

I had a long talk with Rhys when I returned to his place. Things an American might have told me during a first meeting, I had to wait until now to hear from a Scotsman. "I still prefer men in their teens and early twenties," he said, "just the way I did when I was that age myself." I assumed he was in pursuit of Akmal. If so, that was a story the end of which I wouldn't be around to witness, for in the morning I was off to –

LIAM

The Big Smoke, the Black Pool, the city of Joyce and hopefully some Joy as well, namely Dublin. My first host here, Liam, met me at his tram stop accompanied by a golden Labrador retriever. I'd had difficulty finding hosts in Dublin, and to tell the truth, Liam had been among the last batch I'd written to, not liking that he smoked and only had a few references from other surfers. He was in his early sixties, with a white beard and untidy hair.

Liam's house was untidy, too. He told me his vacuum cleaner had died. Standing on the rug before the fireplace, he used his foot to gather up the dog hair on it, then tossed the clump of pale fur onto the grate. He wasn't paying rent on the house, looking after it for an old woman in a nursing home who suffered from dementia. He showed me how to loosen one of the taps on the bathtub after I flushed the toilet. This prevented the pipes from making an anguished moan.

Liam told me he'd become a songwriter in middle age, deciding that was what he most wanted to be. Calling on his experience as a door-to-door salesman, he would knock on people's doors and try to sell them a CD he'd made, or if nothing else get them to listen to him sing a song or two. "If people don't go so far as to buy my album," he said, "usually they at least give me some money for my singing."

Liam was a talking machine. I became a listening machine with him, functioning rather automatically. With the endless talk, the smoking, the dog, the dirty house, the rickety plumbing, I suspected this wasn't going to be my best surf. At least Liam wasn't testy, like Ronen in Tel Aviv, another dog owner. That was the one thing I didn't want to deal with, someone testy.

In the midst of exploring Dublin the next day, I bought a pair of dark blue pants, which allowed me to throw away my old torn pants, also dark blue. What a pleasure to own only one pair at a time! With few choices to make, dressing in the morning was quick and simple, and I always knew where my wallet was.

Liam told me a friend of his, Matteo, was joining us for dinner. The two men had met while working as salesmen. Matteo's landlord was kicking him out, and he planned to move in with Liam. Liam explained the rental program he'd devised. "Matteo will start out paying less than market rate, then at the end of three months, his rent will start to go up like this." He made a gesture of steep ascent. "I'm happy to let Matteo stay with me for a while, to do a friend a favor, but I don't want him dragging out his visit."

My presence apparently delayed the move, for while Matteo arrived with a lot of his possessions, including several oil paintings he'd made and a surfboard, he said he wasn't spending the night, just having dinner with us.

Matteo was in his early thirties. Sketchy beard, bald spot developing on top of his head. He modeled for us a black leather coat he'd found somewhere. "What do you think?" he asked us. Screwing up his face skeptically, Liam asked, "Is that a woman's coat or a man's?" Matteo tried on some of Liam's hats. He had that uncanny Italian ability to look good in all sorts of clothes, even in what might be a woman's coat.

Liam, who talked on and on about his own concerns, had warned me that Matteo would talk on and on about finance. Matteo wanted to buy property in Dublin and so "retire" at thirty-three. By paying in full, he had the advantage of not needing a bank loan, which, as in the U.S., had become difficult to get. "I've already looked at twenty-eight properties," he said with an edge of macho bravado. Liam told him he needed to "shit or get off the pot," an expression Matteo needed Liam to explain. Matteo questioned me about the real estate market in San Francisco. Almost in passing, "Lots of gay people live there, don't they?"

A short while later, Matteo said to me, "You've been traveling a lot. What country do you think has the most beautiful women?" Liam put in, "He isn't the right person to ask." Apparently he'd picked up from my profile that I was gay. Matteo said, "But his view would be more objective," which suggested he'd figured this out, too.

The old sofa-bed in the living room proved reasonably comfortable and the dog reasonably quiet during the night, shut up in the dining room. Liam made me breakfast in the morning, a soupy muesli. Orange juice was his "secret ingredient" in this. I decided this wasn't as bad a surf as it had seemed at first.

Returning to Liam's that evening, I found another surfer had arrived, Ola, a stout Pole with dyed blonde hair. She'd lived most of her adult life in Hamburg, which left her speaking English with a German accent. She'd driven here from Germany, looking for work. I asked why she would consider leaving Germany, which had the strongest economy in Europe. "I'm so tired of the Germans!" she cried. "If they think something is a problem, they obsess about it. A Pole would just say, 'Yes, this is a problem, and we'll try to solve it tomorrow or the day after. But for right now, let's have fun!'" Lowering our voices when Liam was out of the room, Ola and I agreed that Dublin wasn't nearly as beautiful as Edinburgh.

Matteo came to dinner again. I went to a nearby store and bought gnocchi, bread, and an apple tart. Liam made the same sauce for the gnocchi he'd made yesterday for the spaghetti. Ola contributed a bottle of wine. Matteo described in detail a house he was thinking of buying. Ola argued he was looking for a property that would serve two different, possibly contradictory purposes: provide a high rental income and be a good place to live in himself. Her English inadequate to the task, she switched to German a few times, which Matteo for some reason spoke fairly well. During the German passages, Liam would play a game on his mobile, something to do with building a cyber tower with different tenants. I could go along with everything about Liam except his frequent reports about the progress of this stupid tower. Although Matteo and I both told him we didn't want to hear any more about it, he persisted. I reminded myself, At least Liam isn't making us listen to him sing.

ELLIE, JESS, AND GEORGIA

My host in Galway was Ellie, a divorcee with two girls. A surfing first for me, to stay in a household with children. Georgia, the teenager, was away at a sleep-over when I arrived. While the six-year-old, Jess, was at home, she was engrossed in the tellie and whether Harry and Ron could defeat the troll who was smashing up the girl's loo at Hogwarts. This left me to sit at the kitchen table chatting with Ellie. Ellie still possessed a certain amount of prettiness, though her arms had grown thick and the flesh above her breasts was starting to wrinkle. She also had a warm smile that put me at ease. We swapped tales about our Couchsurfing experiences, mine as a guest, hers as a host. I was aware of the potential dangers of this, like talking to someone on a first date about your other dating experiences, not all of which might have been good.

Ellie told me her parents were English. They'd moved to Ireland when she was a child because of the lower cost of living here. She characterized her parents as hippies and pointed out a small oil painting showing them naked. "They were naked a lot," she said. Difficult for me to believe considering Irish weather.

To avoid sending her to a Catholic school, Ellie's parents had home-schooled her, teaming up with some other Protestant parents and their children. "One parent had spent time in France," Ellie said, "so she taught us some French. Another was assigned to teach us math. He was brilliant at math himself, but had no idea how to teach it. I can't even remember what subject my mother taught." The parents had believed children could generate their own education. It shouldn't be imposed by adults as it typically was. "What this mainly boiled down to was lots of hikes in the woods. If we children got excited about an oak tree, an adult would teach us about it. We learned strange things like how to dye wool with onion peelings." Some basics had been neglected, Ellie admitted; her spelling still wasn't very good. Still, she was the only one among this group of children who hadn't gone on to get a university degree.

After exploring Galway the following day, I met Ellie in the town center, along with Jess and Georgia. Georgia had long red hair that she seemed perfectly aware was her best feature. Seeking out glimpses of herself in mirrors and windows, she would rub the sides of her head to make her hair fall in a more fetching way.

The plan had been that we would shop for groceries, which I would pay for. However, Ellie announced she'd found a fifty euro bill on the street that afternoon. "I behaved very well. I stood there for a full ten minutes, holding it, waiting to see if someone would come along scouring the sidewalk, looking for his money. Since no one did, it was clearly a gift from heaven. We're going to spend it on dinner at my favorite restaurant."

I said, "Why don't you let me take you all out for dinner this evening, then you can use your fifty euros for something else later?" Though the cost-counting side of me was thinking, "Oh dear, four dinners will cost more than buying groceries for four people, and I hope her favorite restaurant isn't too expensive."

"No, I absolutely insist," Ellie said. "If you find money on the street, you're supposed to spend it as soon as possible."

"Is that an old Irish custom?"

"No, a new one I just made up."

During the meal, Jess talked a lot, though it was that talk of children that was more like a monologue than part of a real conversation. As for Georgia, she showed me some bracelets she'd bought that day, asking my opinion. Still, most of the time I had the impression she was tuning me out, this middle-aged

American bird of passage her mother was letting sleep on the couch in their living room. Her mind seemed elsewhere, on who could say what, her hair, school, boyfriends, girlfriends?

Well into the dinner, Georgia asked her mother if for her next birthday, she could redecorate her bedroom. "I want to have friends dip their hands in paint and cover the walls with their prints."

I opened my mouth to say something, then closed it again. Georgia hadn't paid much attention to anything else I'd said. Why should I bother to say this? Also, the something was a tiny bit racy, and her mother was sitting right there. Then I said it anyway. What the hell.

"In the Sixties, this artist named Yves Klein had naked female models smear blue paint on themselves, then lie on big sheets of paper to make prints of their bodies."

To my surprise, Georgia looked at me for the first time as if I might be a person who could say something worth listening to. Turning to her mother, she said, "Wouldn't that be cool if we could do that?" I pictured her bedroom walls splashed with blue silhouettes of naked girlfriends and wondered if her mother would thank me for this.

From then on, my stock rose with Georgia. When I said I was going to the loo and told her she needn't come with me and hold my hand as she'd done with Jess, she laughed. Laughter did more to make her pretty than all her hair fussing. When the bill came, Ellie decisively laid down her fifty euro note. I paid the rest, along with a tip. Since this didn't come to much, I took them out for dessert afterward.

As I sat with Ellie in the kitchen after the girls had gone to bed, she talked about her husband, Charlie. "We've been separated for seven months. He's still living in the house we bought. He admits he has a drinking problem, but he hasn't stopped. Hasn't hit rock bottom, the way they say alcoholics need to." Ellie wasn't working, relying on Ireland's good welfare system, which was allowing her to rent a house, run a car.

Charlie had grown up in Zimbabwe, living in a villa with a swimming pool, waited on by servants. He'd expected to inherit the villa, and his parents' lifestyle as well, only to have the family driven out by the civil war, along with most of the other whites. Ellie said, "Charlie has become obsessed with finding footage of the civil war. That seems unhealthy to me." This story made my writer's imagination flare up, the idea of "You can't go home again" applied not to a house or even a town, but an entire country, which in Charlie's case had ceased to exist as he knew it.

I would have liked to hear more about Charlie, and about Ellie's life, and to see if I could build on the connection I'd started to make with Georgia. However, this was one of those speed-dating surfs, where a tight schedule made me move on faster than I wished, after only one full day.

LENKA

My next stay was with Lenka, a pleasant young Romanian woman living in Killarney. I'll only mention it as a cautionary tale. Fellow surfers, always make sure you know your host's address and telephone number. Tattoo them on your arm if necessary. Several conspiring factors – including losing my mobile (which contained Lenka's number) on the bus ride to Killarney and her kindly picking me up at the station in her car rather than making me get to her place on my own – led to my returning in the evening after a bike ride to confront a row of eight identical apartment houses, with four units in each, unsure which door was Lenka's.

I looked through several ground floor windows. This must be Lenka's place, I thought, peering in at one living room. A book about cats lay on the coffee table, and Lenka had a cat. And wasn't that her red couch? Yet the arrangement of the furniture seemed different. . . . I tried the key Lenka had given me in the lock on this front door and that of a few others, without success. A girl leaned out of an upper story window in one building. I worried she would wonder what I was up to and call the police. My uncertainty about which was Lenka's unit crossed with my lack of faith in my ability to open tricky locks.

I decided there was nothing to do but hang around until Lenka returned from her French class at nine. What if I missed her, what was I supposed to do then? Go to the police? What could I tell them? No, sorry, I didn't have the woman's full name or telephone number or exact address. Nor did I have my passport, which was in my luggage inside her house.

Thank God, I did not miss Lenka. Embarrassed by my foolishness, I pretended I was just coming along the street myself. "I had a fantastic bike ride. How was your class?"

RYAN

Cork was my final destination in Ireland. The city looked dreary on a Sunday morning with the streets almost empty. Ryan, my host, whom I'd found in the Gay Ireland group, lived outside Cork in the small town of Passage on the River Lee.

I took the noon bus to Passage; the buses were infrequent on a Sunday. Ryan met me at the bus stop. Hungry, I offered to take him out to lunch at a Chinese restaurant I spotted. I must not have made clear that I intended to pay, for his response was that he didn't have any money. "I won't until tomorrow, when I go to the bank." Even after I clarified, he preferred to eat some soup he'd made and the bread I'd brought.

Ryan seemed nervous. His movements were abrupt. His speech would rush forward, halt, rush forward again. I waited to see what I would make of this, whether it bothered me. After a while, I decided it didn't. Apparently this wasn't a response to me, just his manner.

Ryan asked if I'd seen many signs of Ireland's economic crisis. "Not really," I said. "This is my first trip here, which means I don't have much basis for comparison." Ryan was a city planner, giving him a professional motivation for understanding economic trends. "I knew the country was in a bubble phase five or six years ago," he said, "when housing prices in Dublin were getting way out of line with salaries. Most of my friends dismissed the idea that danger was looming, though."

After the crash, Ryan's salary was cut like that of many civil servants, and more money taken out of what was left to pay for his pension and the like. Encouraged by the Cork city government – "I wouldn't exactly say pressured" – he'd reduced his work week. He was only working three days a week at present, though this did allow him to get to County Mayo to visit his ailing mother without using all his vacation time. He was working to pay off some credit card debt and a bank loan he'd taken out to renovate a house. He'd had to sell the house without recouping the money he'd invested.

Ryan had a cat, Lulu. With her smoky gray fur, she looked like she'd rolled around in soot. "I'm glad I have a cat," Ryan said. "Lulu makes me go to the store to buy cat food, and while I'm there, I buy food for myself. Otherwise I might forget." He never ate out unless someone else was paying. He didn't own a car and had never even taken the bus into town, biking instead no matter what the weather. When I commented on the stacks of books in his living room, he said he didn't want to spend money on bookshelves. I felt myself in a world of money shortage. Ryan's tone wasn't complaining. He seemed to accept his lot, even to find the good in it. Spending less time in the office, he had more for other interests, such as a rowing club and a charity that put troubled youths and drugs addicts to work building boats. He'd moved outside of Cork to have cheaper rent, though his long cycles to work also had the benefit of forcing him to exercise.

"Have you considered emigrating?" I asked Ryan.

"I'm too old at this point," he said. "Anyway, emigrating didn't interest me when I was younger either, going to Australia for example."

My first impression of Passage was that it literally was a "passage," one of those places you used to get from Point A to Point B, but where you didn't linger. I questioned if staying here was one of my surfing mistakes, like staying at the agricultural school on the outskirts of Jerusalem.

Ryan took me on a walk south along a path that used to be a railroad track, following the edge of the river. He pointed out the many shops that had closed. The only type of business the town was well supplied with were pubs, though one of these had shut, too. "I've never gone into any of the pubs," he said. One, the Sirius, apparently had a rough clientele. In the others, he felt he would be a conspicuous outsider, though he'd lived in Passage for almost a year. As Ryan talked about the history of Passage, I saw it as a place where many things *used* to be, before they'd passaged away: railroad, ferry, harbor, dockyards, quay.

We walked through two or three other small towns strung along the water, ones that were a little more affluent-looking and picturesque than Passage. I liked hearing Ryan talk about the buildings we saw, what period they were from. He explained how Cork had become prosperous as the last spot where a ship could take on provisions and passengers before its voyage across the Atlantic.

I was surprised to learn from Ryan that Cork had several gay bars and a sauna. It hadn't looked large enough to sustain these. In the last year, Ryan had only gone to one of the bars a single time, on Gay Pride. He'd organized a gay cycling club for a couple of years, then stopped when only the same people kept taking part. Looking up at the gray sky, which threatened rain, I asked, "Did you cancel the cycling events if the weather was bad?"

"If you did that in Ireland," Ryan replied, "you'd never have any kind of outdoor sports."

Monday, Ryan biked into town to do some things on his day off, while I sat at his kitchen table, using my computer. I'd told him I would probably have a rest day. "You aren't going into Cork?" he said, surprised. This was a day when I was like my father, not wanting to venture far from home, in this case a temporary one. I did go out at last in search of lunch and had a piece of quiche at a surprisingly pleasant cafe next to the Chinese restaurant.

I bought some fruit and veg at a small greengrocers. The owner dropped one elbow onto the counter in a way that communicated he was willing to have a chat.

"Did you watch the Dublin-Kerry match?" he asked.

"No," I said. "Should I be happy Dublin won?"

"I think so," he said, "because it hadn't in sixteen years."

"It probably isn't good for a team to go on winning for too long," I said, "the same way it isn't good for a political party to stay in power too long. My father always said it was better to have a change of party after a while, even if it wasn't to the party you favored."

The owner said darkly, "Things would run better if we didn't have any politicians at all."

I mentioned that several shops near him had closed. "Yes," he said, "people would rather drive to the big supermarkets."

"That's too bad," I said. "No one at Tesco would take the time to chat with a customer the way you are."

I walked south along the river again, in the mood to see things I'd seen before, not something new. I mused on Ryan, on Passage. Could someone be happy here? What would it take? I passed a house with a garden on one side. A lawn behind a high hedge, several rose bushes, a statue, with the greenery of the hillside behind. Would a pretty garden like this be enough to tip the balance?

Ryan didn't return until almost six. I made a salad. He sat on the couch, giving sharp little coughs. These would have soon gotten on my nerves if I'd lived with him. I wondered if he always had this cough. Ryan praised the salad, saying it had been awhile since he'd eaten anything this healthy. Encouraged by me, he talked about Irish history, languages. The more we talked, the more I was struck by his range of knowledge. Yet that initial impression of a sad life in a sad small town persisted. He'd referred to himself several times as old, though according to his profile, he was only fifty, younger than I was. I wanted to ask if he was dating someone. The conversation kept to less personal subjects. In any case, I assumed the answer was no.

I once read a book by an American colonial woman captured by Native-Americans. Living in their village, learning to gather food and make clothes in their way, she kept trying to make sense of her new circumstances through references to the Good Book. "I repaired to my Bible (my great comfort in that time) and that scripture came to my hand, 'Cast thy burden on the Lord, and He shall sustain thee.'" The Bible doesn't serve me as a lens as it did this Puritan. However, I did spend a lot of time as a kid listening to those five musicals stored in a cupboard in my parents' dining room. Trying to help foreigners get a grip on my first name, I say, "Have you ever heard that song about Gary, Indiana?" (*The Music Man*). Whenever I think about a hateful boss I once had, my mind launches into that sublime vengeance song, "Just You Wait!" (*My Fair Lady*). Put catchy words to catchy music, and they will stay lodged in someone's brain for the rest of his life.

Scene: an elementary school in Ubud, Bali. I'd come here to see Kayla, a young American woman I'd met on the drive from Amed to Ubud. Kayla was a counterculture type, full of projects like writing a children's book about permaculture. Wherever she had an extended stay in her travels, she found volunteer work to do. In Ubud, she was teaching English to children at this four-room school run by a Dutch couple. On the drive, she'd invited me to visit her there. Unfortunately when I arrived, the Dutch woman, Evi, told me Kayla was sick that day and hadn't been able to come. "Do you want to teach the class?" Evi smiled.

I looked at the ten children sitting on benches at communal desks. "I'm sorry, I wouldn't know how."

Evi took my refusal graciously. "You're welcome to observe the class for a while if you like, since you're here," she said, gesturing toward the back of the room. She worked on the days of the week with the children, the names for different body parts. They laughed at the bad drawings she made on the blackboard of an arm, an ear.

Later, Evi approached me. "Could you at least teach the children a game or a song, just for a quarter-hour? I have some things I need to do in the office."

"I guess I can teach them a song," I said, "if I can remember the words."

While Evi spent a few more minutes with the students on such peculiarities as saying "teeth" instead of "tooths," I went to the blackboard. Yes, all the words came back to me. Not that there were many. One of the secrets of the song's memorability was that there were so few.

So there in Bali if not in Thailand, in shorts and T-shirt if not in hoop skirt and petticoat, I pointed with a ruler from one word to the next on the blackboard and sang as best I could "Getting to Know You." I love this song because it affirms that getting to know a new person will most likely be a rewarding experience. If I were compiling a Songbook for Travelers, I would make this the very first piece.

The kids appeared to enjoy singing it, giggling at their mistakes. At least this was more fun than trying to fathom "teeth" instead of "tooths."

Chapter 8

Atlantic Seaboard: Follies

ADRIEN

"Welcome back," said the man at the customs desk in Dulles airport. After many examinations of my passport at borders and questions about travel plans and even means of support, it was pleasant to arrive in a place where an official simply said, "Welcome back."

I thought I'd been lucky with my host in Washington, D.C. Adrien was French, and I looked forward to getting the French perspective on the U.S. He lived within walking distance of the Mall, in what looked from the photographs in his profile like a swanky apartment.

When I arrived in the lobby of his building, a concierge telephoned Adrien. A concierge! Usually I was just pressing a buzzer and hoping it was actually making a sound in my host's apartment, or using a knocker on a door, or my knuckles. Adrien came down in the elevator. He didn't offer to help me with my luggage. At the time, I simply noticed this as untypical of hosts. Later I saw it as a warning that I might not have been as lucky as I supposed.

The apartment had a characterless look, as if it had been rented furnished. Cat hair on the two couches. Cat litter on the bathroom floor. After I'd been in the apartment a short while, Adrien asked me to take off my shoes, making me feel I'd erred by walking around in them. Adrien forty according to his profile, with one of those bodies that appeared to melt as the person aged, losing its sharp outline and firmness. He had a particular way of gesturing, rotating his hands from flexible wrists, which I liked. I liked his voice, too, his French accent.

Adrien's two small cats were flopped on the L-shaped couch. They looked like they had more fur than flesh. "The cats are my babies," Adrien said. "They're purebred Persians." He pulled at the fur of Ida, the young female, untangling it. "My last surfer was from San Francisco, too. The cats *loved* him for some reason. They followed him around." I looked at the cats, and they looked at me, and we neither loved nor hated.

"You're a writer," Adrien said.

"Yes," I said. "And so are you."

Adrien stated in his profile that he was writing a book. This turned out to be his autobiography. "I've already written eighty thousand words, and I've still only reached the age of twenty-five." In answer to my question, he said he was writing the book entirely from memory, without any help from journals or other materials. He claimed he could remember things clearly from age one.

"I plan to publish the book myself," Adrien said. "I don't want to deal with publishers, all their criticisms. I just want to put it out there and see if people would like to read it. That would be enough for me. I'm not interested in making money from it. Though who knows, maybe someone will turn it into a movie."

I said, "I think most people have at least one good book in them. If nothing else, the story of their lives."

"My story is unique," Adrien said. I took this to mean, Other people may write the story of their commonplace lives; mine is of special interest.

Sweeping away any notions that Europeans were more reticent than Americans, Adrien launched into his unique story. His mother hadn't liked him, he said, hadn't wanted him. What about his father? I asked. No, his father hadn't liked him either. "My mother was rigid and authoritarian, my father shy and introverted. My sister was like our mother. She conformed, so she got along better with our parents."

Adrien went on, "At four, I refused to eat meat." Having struggled through a month long trip in meat-oriented France in a period when I was a vegetarian, I could imagine this hadn't gone over well. "I've always liked animals, and I didn't want to be responsible for hurting them. A nurse who looked after my sister and me once made us horse meat for lunch. My sister ate it. I refused. The nurse told me I would sit there at the table until I ate it. I cried, but still said no. Finally, when I was twelve, I did start eating meat. Though never horse meat!"

I said something about the family dynamics in my play. "I've written plays, too," Adrien said. I sensed a tendency for one-upmanship. You've written a play, and so have I.

I asked Adrien if his plays had been staged. "No, I wrote them all when I was still a teenager and performed them with my friends." At least this added a rare fun note to what sounded like a not very fun childhood.

Adrien asked if I wanted to use the jacuzzi. From his window, we could see it on a lower rooftop of the building.

"Sure," I said. This was one of the things I wanted to learn from Couchsurfing, to say yes to ideas like this that dropped out of the sky. We discovered that the jacuzzi wasn't switched on. Descending to the lobby, Adrien asked the concierge why. He was brusque, didn't smile. "I'll call someone else in the building to see what the problem is," she said politely.

We returned to the terrace, where Adrien swam in the small pool near the jacuzzi. The concierge appeared and told him a serviceman had been called. She hoped the jacuzzi would be working by tomorrow. From the pool, Adrien stared at her, still unsmiling. I could tell he was about to say something like, "It's the responsibility of the building to have the jacuzzi working at all times." He refrained.

I offered to take Adrien out to dinner. On the street, he walked quickly, and since he was taller than I was, I had trouble keeping up with him. He led me to a restaurant that he said Trip Adviser had given the highest rating in D.C. The maîtresse d' said we would have to wait an hour and a half for a table. I was relieved, since from the look of the place, the prices were clearly also high.

I pointed out a neon sign for a Cuban restaurant farther up the street. Cuba was a poor country, so surely a restaurant offering Cuban food would be inexpensive. Stepping into an elaborate stage set of Old Havana, with fans turning overhead and fake flowering vines climbing the walls, I suspected my reasoning was faulty.

In our exchange of messages before I arrived in D.C., Adrien had seized on my describing myself in my profile as a bon vivant. "You like wine?" he asked once we were seated in the restaurant. "And maybe cigars?" I disabused him on both points, apologizing.

"Would a French bon vivant necessarily drink wine?" I asked.

"Yes," Adrien replied.

It appeared I wasn't the sort of person he'd expected, and he wasn't what I had.

I ordered the vegetarian ravioli, the man who wouldn't eat horse meat, a steak. Adrien had a long interaction with our black waitress about how the steak should be cooked. I took this as good service. That was something all foreigners agreed the U.S. offered, good service.

Time passed, and our dinners didn't appear. Adrien flagged down a waiter and complained. More time passed. He flagged down another waitress, flopping his hand from the wrist with increased agitation. Still no results. Our waitress seemed to have vanished. I said, "I wish we had a rude French waiter who was at least efficient."

At last our waitress reappeared. From complete neglect, she switched to too much talk, a lengthy apology. "Just before I took your order, my sister called to say our uncle had died." Her story would have made more sense if the call had come *after* she'd taken the order: she was so upset, she forgot to send it in, or something like that. She assured us, "I'm a medical student, which means I know how important it is for people to eat." A bus boy brought us free plantain chips and a free glass of wine for Adrien. I thought, I guess that's good American service, freebies when the service has been bad.

Our talk returned to Adrien's parents. "I visit them once a year," he said. "My father doesn't ask me anything about my life, even though I'm living abroad and doing interesting work at the World Bank. I have to ask about what *he* is doing, this retired man. Ask about his gardening."

"This is probably a very American thing to say," I ventured, "but what if you told your father, 'I feel bad about some of the things that happened when I was a kid, and I'd like to talk to you about them'?"

"My father wouldn't even understand. Besides, it's too late. I can't complain about these things so long afterward, when I'm forty. If I told my father I was gay – I just can't imagine how he'd react."

I wondered if Adrien only meant this hypothetically. A short while later, I asked if he was enjoying the dating scene in D.C. He mentioned dating both men and women. "Being gay is becoming more acceptable in the West," he said, "but not being bisexual. People want me to say I'm on this side or that side." Adrien had had four girlfriends in his life and four boyfriends, which did suggest he was equally poised between the two worlds. None of the relationships had lasted more than six months. He seemed a little chagrined to admit this. Recently he'd dated a woman, paying for their nights out. Then the woman had sent an email saying she didn't think they were compatible. "She broke up with me by email. That was very rude. You can at least have a last coffee with someone."

Adrien took another sip of his free glass of wine. "I'm equally attracted to men and women, but I do find women more cruel. And they expect you to pay for everything! Men are easier. I understand them better, being a man myself. Still, these days my age is making me more interested in women because I want to have children. What about you? Are you attracted to women?"

"No," I said. Was I again disappointing?

Back at the apartment, I touched on the Key Question. For me as probably for other surfers, the Key Question was a key question: would the host give me one or not? If a host stated in his profile that he didn't lend a key, I probably wouldn't send him a request, not unless I was only staying one night or he worked from home and could let me in and out. If I could avoid it, I didn't want to be sent off to nine-to-five tourism while the host was sent off to his nine-to-five job. What if I was sick, or tired, or just wanted to dawdle in the morning?

If I didn't know where a host stood on the Key Question beforehand, I hoped at least to have this clarified during my visit in a way that wasn't awkward. As so often in this stay, awkwardness prevailed. I asked Adrien if he needed me to leave with him in the morning. This is a sub-question of the Key Question. "If you don't," he replied, "you'd need to have a key." "Can I just close the door behind me when I leave?" I said. He didn't respond. I had an aunt with this annoying habit, simply failing to respond when I asked her something she didn't care to be asked. I assumed in this case that silence was non-consent.

As we were about to leave the apartment together the next morning, Adrien said, "You're wearing shorts," giving them a disapproving look. I thought, "It's a hot, sticky June day, and I'll be walking around outside, not sitting in an air-conditioned office, so yes, I'm wearing shorts." Once we parted on the street, I realized my shoulders were scrunched up with tension. Instead of heading straight for the Mall as I'd planned, I sat down on the first bench I could find. Needing to decompress with a little non-Adrien time, I spent the next ten minutes breathing quietly, my eyes on the ground.

When I returned to the apartment at the end of the day, Adrien and I set off again for the jacuzzi. This time it was working and, at the end of a tropical day, a number of people were using it or lying around the pool. They were all young, probably students at Georgetown's law school nearby; Adrien said most of the tenants in the building were students there. Two men sat next to each other, one with his baseball cap on backward, the other with it facing front. Absent from the country for a long time, I must have missed a memo explaining that every American man, woman, and child, regardless of age, would be issued a baseball cap. A man ordered take-out on his mobile, half lounging on a lounge chair. He gave the impression of someone young enjoying the new role of affluent adult, ordering food, asking for extra dressing for the salad. A couple in the jacuzzi, the guy's arm around the shoulders of the girl. A man reading a law book, headphones on. A biography of Steve Jobs left on one chair.

Adrien swam in the pool while I sat waiting for him, a little awkward; our age made us the odd men out. Entering the jacuzzi, he sat between the couple and the steps so there wasn't room for me to sit beside him, which seemed strange. Far apart, we hardly spoke. I had a view of the Capitol Building. This had the air of a caption on a Facebook photo: "Here I am in a jacuzzi with a view of the Capitol Building!" A moment you didn't value as much for itself as how it could be packaged.

Back in the apartment, I complimented Adrien on the blue shirt he put on. "Did you buy that in Paris?" I asked.

"No, here," he said, a little snappish. "Why do you ask?"

I thought, To make conversation. I said, "Because I like it."

"I have this same shirt in purple, too. I wore it yesterday. Don't you remember?" We'd gone from my paying him a compliment to my being at fault for not remembering the purple version.

As if not quite giving up on the idea of me as a fellow bon vivant, Adrien suggested we have dinner at a cigar bar. I agreed, again wanting to say yes to new experiences. One wall of the bar was lined with wooden drawers containing different cigars. Television screens wherever I looked showed a baseball game. This elicited periodic whoops from the almost entirely male crowd.

Adrien had said he always met men in cigar bars, another thing that encouraged me to go along with the idea. Entering, he asked whether I wanted to sit at a table or on the two rows of couches facing each other. "Where are we more likely to meet men?" I asked. "On the couches," he said. I flickered between seeing Adrien as gay and straight, which was interesting. "We might meet some guys," I said. I added, "Or you might meet a woman."

Two husky black men sat down on one of the couches across from us and to our left. They ordered hamburgers, didn't look at us. After a time, it seemed clear we probably weren't going to meet *them*. Nor the two white guys to our right sprawled in big armchairs, engrossed in their mobiles. Studying the menu, Adrien complained, "The problem with Couchsurfers is they usually don't have much money. It makes it hard to go out to nice places with them."

I asked Adrien about his experiences with other surfers. He told me about a Brazilian man he'd hosted while living in Paris. "Mino was supposed to stay for a week. Then he asked if he could stay longer. He ended up staying seventeen days, until at last I told him to leave. Mino was very attractive. He was trying to become a model. I'm sure he was using his looks to find places to surf." Adrien complained that Mino "used his things," though the only one he specified was his WiFi.

"I wrote Mino a negative reference," Adrien said. "He responded by writing a negative one for me, claiming I'd made advances, which wasn't true. He told me he'd remove his reference if I removed mine."

"And did you?" I asked.

"Yes," Adrien said. "He had me in a corner." So much for the incontestable value of Couchsurfing references.

Adrien held out his mobile toward me. "Look," he said proudly, "the Couchsurfer who stayed with me before you just left me my hundredth reference."

The food service went without a hitch on this occasion. However, when it came time for Adrien to order a cigar – well, I'm sure by now the reader can finish this story himself with something suitable.

I was leaving for Philadelphia the next morning as part of a crawl up the East Coast. Parting from Adrien on the street, with him on the way to work and me to Union Station, he asked if I would write him a reference. I thought, You already have a hundred references. Why does it matter to you to have a hundred-and-first?

Nevertheless, having been raised with a modicum of good manners, I agreed to leave him one. With some time to kill while waiting for my train, I got the business over with using my laptop and the WiFi at a coffee shop in the station. "You're a writer," I told myself. "You should be able to come up with a reference that's acceptable to Adrien while not misleading to people considering him as a host." I did manage to scrape something together, though it didn't include, "Had a wonderful time."

Within ten minutes of posting the reference, I saw that Adrien in turn had left one for me. Maybe he'd said the same thing to himself about being a good writer and so on, because he'd made his reference similarly bland. For the most part at any rate. He did slip in, "Gary doesn't drink wine or smoke, and he's very frugal." In other words, I was a Puritanical skinflint.

No matter. My train was about to board, and literally and figuratively, it was time to move on.

TYLER, SILVANA, TYLER, JR., AND ABUELA

Arriving in Philadelphia, I checked my luggage at the train station and set off to explore the city. Passing a hostel at one point, still feeling surf-shocked by my stay with Adrien, I was tempted to check in. How nice it would be to come and go as I pleased, not to have to talk with anyone, to eat at cheap restaurants.

Returning to the station late in the afternoon, I took a regional train through an area filled with many mingy townhouses. Finally out to a succession of more salubrious suburban towns. I got off at a cute old-fashioned station. "Welcome to Abington Township" read a sign at the exit to the parking lot. "Please Watch Our Children." I gathered this meant, "Watch out for our children if you're driving," though there were other possibilities. I wheeled my suitcase past big wood-framed houses with front porches. I thought, If I were content to live out in a pretty suburb like this and never venture into the gritty center, I might consider moving to an East Coast city.

My hosts were a family living in a church that the husband, a builder, had turned into condominiums. I knocked on the door of their unit. Nothing happened, though I could hear people inside. Knocked louder. Finally, a ten-year-old boy opened the door.

"Hi, I'm Gary, I'm Couchsurfing here, with Tyler. Can I speak with your grandmother?" Tyler had told me that the *abuela* at least would be home.

"She can't speak English," the boy said.

"I can speak Spanish with her." Considering the quality of my Spanish, this was optimistic.

Abuela, a short elderly woman, gave the impression she wasn't expecting me, or maybe half-expecting. After a few minutes, Silvana, Tyler's wife, appeared. I'd told Adrien I wasn't attracted to women. Still, I knew a bombshell when I saw one and could feel at least some of the effect. Thirty, black hair, big eyes, breasts she would have been a fool not to take pride in.

Her skimpy red silk robe suggested she was not a fool. I was careful not to drop my eyes from her face, gathering there was nothing between her breasts and the silk.

Silvana showed me my room upstairs and gave me a towel. Her manner was brisk. Back in the kitchen, she asked, "Do you want something to eat?" "Sure," I said. Silvana was about to serve me a large piece of pork out of a stew pot. I said, "I don't need such a big piece. A smaller one is fine." She said, "No, you want this piece. You'll like it." I sat at the counter to eat the pork, along with some sliced cucumbers dressed with vinegar.

Silvana spoke with an accent. "Where do you come from?" I asked.

"Cuba," she said.

I said, "That's funny. On my train ride this morning, I was thinking about how I want to visit Cuba." I didn't add that one of my motives was to search for man-to-man romance beneath the Caribbean moon.

Tyler appeared. In his profile, he'd looked rather handsome, in a rangy American way. In person, he was putting on weight, and age or stress was eroding the handsomeness.

We chatted. Tyler told me how he and Silvana had met. "A driver picked me up while I was hitchhiking in Cuba. That's the philosophy in a communist country: you help other people. Later the driver picked up Silvana, too. She was visiting her father, who lived in Havana. She had a headache, and I gave her something for it – I had good meds! The driver suggested I ask her out to dinner, and she gave me her number."

"I didn't think he would call," Silvana smiled, "but he did."

Romance blossomed. Tyler traveled to Cuba often. In the end, he racked up almost thirty visits. He had permission from the U.S. government to travel there, he didn't explain to me why. On one visit, Silvana presented Tyler with his baby son.

He told her he would take care of them. Tyler already had a girlfriend in Philadelphia, Lenore, an Aussie. He thought he could lead separate lives with the two women. Later, Lenore had a child, Nicole, who was now five. This two-family story reminded me of that of Daniel in Cologne.

For reasons that still weren't clear to Tyler, the Cuban government later barred him from entering the country. Silvana was miserable that Tyler couldn't visit her anymore. Without telling him about her plan, she managed to get on a speedboat with other refugees and reach the U.S. She called Tyler from Florida to say she'd arrived. She didn't speak English at that point and later had to learn the language.

Tyler brought Silvana to the town of three hundred in West Virginia where he'd grown up. Surprise, Mom and Dad, here's my Cuban girlfriend and son! "My mom almost had a heart attack," Tyler told me. "My dad took it better." Tyler later gave Lenore the same surprise. "Tyler," I laughed, "the next time you want to surprise someone, get my advice first." Later, Abuela had come to the States for a "visit," then never returned to Cuba, moving in with them instead.

Tyler admitted he'd thought the households of the two mothers would get along. He'd renovated a condo nearby, a nicer one in an even better area, and told Lenore she could have it if she agreed to live there until their daughter was eighteen. Mistake. "Ever since I gave Lenore the condo, she's been trying to figure out how to sell it so she can move back to Australia and take Nicole with her."

Tyler had wrangled in court with Lenore to the tune of fifty thousand dollars in legal fees. He'd wanted to get the unsold condos in the church on the spring market, then was too busy dealing with the court. Lenore had acquired a new boyfriend, who was a family law attorney.

"What bad luck!" I exclaimed.

"It wasn't, actually," Tyler said. "She's done worse in court ever since she started taking his advice."

Still, Tyler was allowed only a fifth of Nicole's time. "Lenore questions Nicole after every visit to me, looking for things she can object to in court." Tyler conveyed that I wouldn't meet Nicole tomorrow when she came over. He didn't want her mother to know he was having Couchsurfers stay in the house – "strangers."

Tyler explained how he'd started hosting surfers. "My dad was my inspiration. He used to pick up hitchhikers. Sometimes he even brought them home to spend the night. I admired him for doing that and want to carry on the tradition."

Of all my hosts, Tyler seemed the most altruistic in his motives. Although willing to talk with me when he had time, he wasn't someone who craved an audience, nor did he want me to entertain him or educate him. He needed nothing from me.

Tyler marked up my Philly map, advising me where to go tomorrow. He even loaned me a pass to the art museum. Having said he needed to diet, he proceeded to fill a huge bowl with ice cream which he heaped with fruit salad Abuela had made. He urged me to have some ice cream, too. I accepted a half scoop. "You clearly want to stay thin," Tyler smiled, his one and only personal remark. He took his dessert up to his office, saying he needed to do some more work. If I were his friend, I thought, I'd tell him not to work so hard and to look after himself more.

I only had a glimpse of Tyler the next morning when he appeared in bathrobe, slippers, and knit cap, and went outside to talk to a couple of men doing work on the building. The Cuban bombshell appeared in black body suit with a belt of silver metal circles. "Do you have a gay brother I can visit while I'm in Cuba?" I wanted to ask.

Silvana had Abuela make me oatmeal. Silvana said she didn't like American breakfasts. In Cuba, people only ate coffee and a roll, which was what she had now. She put some of the fruit salad in a plastic container to eat for lunch at her school. "I'm studying Management," she told me. "I want to open a small business, maybe a Cuban restaurant. Philadelphia only has a few of those. I don't want to stay home all day. That would drive me crazy."

I looked out the kitchen window at the adjacent yards. "Do you know your neighbors?" I asked.

"No," Silvana said. "I hardly even see them. The woman in the house behind us used to be friends with Tyler. She works in a bakery, and she'd bring him pastries. Then I arrived! I think she was in love with Tyler and jealous of me. She and Tyler got into an argument over a fence he built between their properties. He agreed to move it finally, but now they aren't speaking to each other."

"This place must be so different from Cuba," I said.

"Yes." Silvana talked a little about her village, the plaza where everyone would mingle, talk, dance. "Cuba is stuck in the past. It's fifty years behind. But I do think people are happier there."

Couchsurfing was clearly Tyler's project, which Silvana probably saw as yet another odd American idea (Couchsurfing is essentially illegal in Cuba, where a host would have to inform the authorities about each guest or risk a fine). On my arrival, she'd told me, "This is your house" without investing this statement with much feeling. Still, that didn't make it hypocritical or meaningless. I gathered she took my visit in stride, as she accepted that the three-year-old son of the couple living below them arrived to spend the day being looked after by Abuela. I conjectured a non-American acceptance of sharing her space with others, family, friends, some Couchsurfer, the neighbor's child. Having me here was her husband's idea, yet she'd still insisted I have the bigger piece of pork. While Silvana might be indifferent to me, I couldn't help liking her and admiring her spunk. She must have felt isolated there in Abington Township where residents asked you to watch their children.

Silvana's isolation seemed nothing compared with Abuela's, with her complete lack of English. After Silvana left, I used my limited Spanish to chat with her as she sat at the kitchen table, making dolls out of recycled fabric. I managed to get that the hair on one doll had come from the yarn she'd unpicked from an old sweater. "In Cuba," she said, "we don't throw anything away. We can't, we're too poor." Abuela marveled at how much more affluent the U.S. was. "This big refrigerator! I bought one in Cuba that's like this" (she gestured to show one a third the size) "and it was very expensive." She said she'd met only a few people in the area who spoke Spanish.

Tyler had mentioned one other motivation for hosting, that he wanted Tyler, Jr. to meet people from other parts of the world, as he himself had done in his parents' home. Returning from a day of sightseeing, I tried to earn my keep by asking Junior to show me around the building, something his father had suggested. Junior led me through several unfinished units, all cleverly inserted into the old church space.

"Your English is perfect," I said. "Do you remember not speaking English when you arrived in the U.S.?"

"Yeah," Junior said, "but at this point, I know I speak it well. Only I do have some trouble with reading and writing."

A pause, with me wondering what else one talked about with a ten-year-old.

"Do you want to be a builder like your dad when you grow up?" I asked.

"No," Junior said decisively.

The tour over, Junior plunked himself back in his armchair in the living room and resumed his video game, displayed on a large screen. Although cheerful and apparently well-adjusted, this seemed to be the only thing Junior wanted to do, like Pavel in Jerusalem: play video games. Giving up on my role as the horizon-broadening guest, I joined Abuela in the kitchen, where she was watching a peppy Spanish-language game show on another television.

ETHAN

The musical featured in this chapter is so quintessentially New York that I've waited until my arrival in that city to introduce it: Stephen Sondheim's *Follies*. *The King and I* came into my life very early, *Follies* not until middle age. This is another no-movie musical and another I've never seen on stage. I've always regretted not attending a production playing in Madrid during one of my visits, thus missing out on Carlotta Campion singing, "*Todavia estoy aqui*." For me, this is chiefly an audio musical, introduced to me by my ex's CD. By careful searching on YouTube, I once pieced together a weird Frankenstein *Follies* from many different sources. Still, most of the snippets were from concerts and nightclub acts, not staged productions. As a result, I don't have much visual sense of the piece, nor much grasp of the story beyond the basic premise: some old song and dance folk attend a reunion in a condemned Broadway theater where they performed together between the wars, and presumably have some last-act catharsis. In my mind, *Follies* exists more like a big songbook, containing both of-the-moment numbers (the moment being the early Seventies) and pastiches covering a big swath of the history of the American musical.

Appropriate that a musical with the theme "I used to be young and I'm not anymore" played a part in my middle age. After breaking up with my ex, I was launched again into singlehood after a sixteen year hiatus. San Francisco offers a single man lots of choices of things to do, and I did some of them. Still, I wondered if I could offer single guys something better, or at least different, something with my personal stamp on it. I decided to give an Eligible Bachelor Party at my house.

The party was a success and my house survived pretty well, except for some discarded name tags stuck to the hardwood floors and a towel rack yanked off the bathroom wall when one newly-minted couple was in too much of a hurry to become intimate. Needing more space, I moved on to a mansion owned by an elderly man in my writers' critique group. Finally, losing the homey touch but making life simpler for me, I held the next few parties at Mecca, a restaurant and bar on Market Street. I chose Mecca because it was large, had pretensions to class, and was strangely empty much of the time and therefore eager to boost business.

I gave each party a theme. For "Being Single is a Drag," I gave the guests both a name tag and a "drag tag" with a drag name: Penny Tration, Lotta Gaul, Kitten Kaboodle, Miss Understood. Entertainment was provided by several drag queens. "When You're Single, At Least There's Porn" featured two porn stars. They were surprisingly wholesome, a couple living in Sacramento, who said they only performed in films together. One acquaintance told me he found this theme offensive. I believe he attended in any case.

The theme for what turned out to be the last party was "Single Life is a Cabaret." I wanted to find a singer and choose the songs performed. I got it into my head to write my own lyrics to "Broadway Baby" from *Follies*, transformed into "Single Baby." If gay Stephen Sondheim refused to write songs about gay people himself, he'd have to accept some help from me.

To be continued, since I've arrived at the building of my New York host, Ethan, and rung the bell. . . .

Too much to hope that Ethan would live in a derelict Broadway theater. Instead, he offered a Hell's Kitchen loft that had once been a garment factory. "Ascending into hell," I mused on the elevator ride up.

Ethan opened his door accompanied by a hailstorm of yaps from two small dogs. Ethan was in his late seventies, short. I assumed he'd always been short, though old-age shrinkage might have made him even shorter. He was a study in black and white, his hair white, eyebrows still black, mustache a mix of the two. I was old enough myself to remember mustaches from the early Eighties and asked myself if Ethan had held on to his continuously since then.

I presented Ethan with a box of cereal I'd bought on the walk from the bus station. Although I planned to take him out to dinner, I was playing it safe. I'd had fair warning he wouldn't be an easy-going host from his profile, which included a long list of rules for surfers, including a midnight curfew. Surfers should give him a thank you present, he said, "at least a box of cereal."

Showing me around the loft, Ethan explained he'd bought it thirty years ago, putting in the kitchen and bathrooms, the interior walls. The new Comfort Inn slammed up against Ethan's building ten years ago had blocked almost half his side windows, though that still left an unbroken succession across the front. Ethan had a loft-mate, Todd, who was on holiday in Mexico at the moment. "I met Todd even before I met my ex," Ethan said. "People think we're lovers, that I'm using 'roommate' as a euphemism. But we aren't and never were." There was apparently only one ex, though with all Ethan's talk, I never heard much about him except that he'd died of AIDS in the early years of the epidemic.

Ethan was a former real estate loan officer. "I thought you used to be an actor," I said, trying to remember his profile. Ethan told me he'd done some acting, too, as part of Charles Ludlam's Ridiculous Players. "Then I realized being an actor meant I couldn't go to the theater myself, because if you're an actor, you're usually tied up in the evening with your own work."

Looking around the enormous loft, I thought of the poor slobs paying large sums to rent no doubt quite small rooms in the hotel next door. Ethan told me he'd had a disco party here in the early Eighties with two hundred guests, and I could easily picture the space accommodating that many. There were two bathrooms, a big kitchen area, a truly vast living area. So much space in fact that it seemed to have exhausted Ethan and Todd's interior design abilities. The loft had an air of incompletion, of a place where things had been set down temporarily, then for some reason never moved into a final and logical position. The area beyond the dining table was like a used furniture store, with stuff heaped together, a sideboard, a hat rack, an old Budweiser sign. Opera music played on the radio. "That's Luciano Pavarotti," Ethan said, "who died too young."

The living area was dominated by a white leather couch in the form of a circle with one quarter removed; dominated to the extent any single piece of furniture could in such a large space. Ethan had some other surfers staying with him besides me. He was mad at Jan, the young German, for leaving his rumpled sheets on the couch. His other guests, he referred to as "a sweet Slovenian couple," until he discovered the man was drying the T-shirts and underwear he'd laundered on the doors to the cupboards that lined the front of the loft. "I told him I had a dryer," Ethan groused, snatching up the damp clothing. "Didn't he stop to think this might damage the wood?"

I accompanied Ethan on a walk with the dogs. He had to walk them four times a day while Todd was in Mexico. He let me hold the leash of the friendlier dog, which I referred to privately as Fluffy. The dogs were old, like Ethan, and Fluffy's pink tongue hung out perpetually following some dental work. "Don't let her eat garbage," Ethan warned. How was I to distinguish fast enough between her eating off the pavement and sniffing it?

Ethan told me some surfers tales. One about two Russian guys who were cycling across the U.S. The taller Russian had smelled. "First, I suggested he take a shower. No, he said. Next, that he let me wash his clothes. No. Then I offered him an extra deodorant I had. No, again. Finally on the last day of his visit, I sprayed him with bathroom cleaner. He got so mad!"

Ethan had surfers coming and going in the loft all the time; a sort of professional host like Rhys in Edinburgh. He said French surfers were often rude, had attitude. Russians: arrogant know-it-alls. Asians: strange eating habits, and their English often poor. He didn't want to host children, or even teenagers, since they weren't good conversationalists. "This Chinese couple with a baby sent me a request. I told them no. 'It's a good baby,' they wrote back, 'it doesn't cry much.' Not *much!*" Ethan told me what he considered good gifts from surfers, things like cologne, chocolate, wine. Bad ones, things like key rings or refrigerator magnets. "I don't want you to think I'm an old curmudgeon," Ethan said. No, I thought, of course not.

Soon after I returned from a day of nibbling on the Big Apple, Jan showed up. He had hair that was long enough to tie in back, a body clearly the product of working out. Not surprising to find he was getting a degree in sports management. Ethan brought Jan over to his rumpled sheet like a dog that had peed indoors. "Didn't your mother teach you to make your bed? Stay in a hotel if you want to leave it like this all day." Jan had shown "disrespect."

While Ethan was out walking the dogs again, I asked Jan if he'd gotten him a present. No, he said. I suggested he do so.

I was determined to avoid getting scolded by Ethan myself. Perhaps inevitably, this was not to be. Ethan had left the television news on. Jan asked me if we could turn off the sound. Examining the remote, we found the mute button. Ethan returned while Jan was in the bathroom. "Where's the sound?" he demanded, standing in front of the screen. I explained what had happened, the hot water I was in not cooled by my inability to find the mute button immediately to restore the sound. "I was only gone ten minutes! I wish people wouldn't touch my things!"

When Jan appeared, he offered to clean the bathrooms as a thank you present, since he didn't have a lot of money. Ethan leered, "You can do it in the nude. There are people who do that in New York, you know, clean in the nude. A lot of horny men here."

Jan told Ethan and me about his visit to a tattoo artist in the East Village that afternoon. The artist had already completed the first stage of a tattoo on Jan's back in Berlin. At present the peripatetic artist was in New York, and Jan had taken advantage of his own visit here to receive the second stage. "Show it to us," Ethan said. Jan obliged, pulling up his T-shirt in back. I could see why this tattoo had to be done in stages, for it filled Jan's large back from top to bottom and side to side. Odin rode a horse with eight legs, with a couple of wolves racing along below. The top third was just an outline, waiting to be filled in.

"Let me take a picture for the guest book," Ethan said, grabbing his camera. The guest book lay on the coffee table, filled with photographs of young men caught with their shirts off, sometimes in nothing but their underwear. "Turn around and I'll get a shot of you from the front," Ethan ordered, though Jan didn't have a tattoo there.

I took Ethan out to dinner at a nearby Chinese restaurant. The waitress practically tossed our empty plates on the table, one of them nudging my tea cup and making it spill. Ethan exchanged a communicative glance with me. We did have these moments when we were a little like friends.

I heard about Ethan's background. Grew up in Brooklyn. Father from Turkey via Romania. Mother from Ukraine via Israel. Two brothers. I heard the most about Caleb, the next oldest after Ethan. Caleb was irresponsible, liked to gamble.

Their mother wrote a will dividing the estate equally among the three brothers. Later, in the type of not-leaving-well-enough-alone decision that lawyers were eternally grateful for, she added Ethan as a joint holder on all her bank accounts, fearing the two younger brothers would otherwise run through their inheritance. The mother's lawyer told Ethan this action superseded the terms of the will. In control of the estate assets after their mother's death, Ethan doled out money to Caleb when he needed it, to pay income tax or medical bills, to fix his car.

"I thought I handled this well. I didn't say to him things like, 'Shouldn't you have been saving for this?' Finally, Caleb asked for his share of the estate, the whole thing. I said no. He sent our email correspondence to all our relatives and friends, trying to blacken my name. He even sent it to my dentist."

Caleb told Ethan he didn't want any further contact with him. "You're as dead to me!" Ethan cut Caleb out of his will, and his children, too, since they'd cold-shouldered him at their father's orders.

Later in the evening, Tana and Dario, the Slovenian couple, returned to the loft. Tana enthused, "People in New York are so polite! Everywhere we go, in shops, restaurants, on the street."

Jan came to me and asked if I could put ointment on his tattoo and cover it with plastic wrap, to protect the tattoo and keep his skin from drying out. I assumed he saw me as a safer bet than Ethan. Performing this operation in the bathroom, patting on the ointment, stretching sheets of plastic wrap across Jan's back, I thought, If I were staying in stupid Comfort Inn, I probably wouldn't be doing anything as memorable as this, just watching the boob tube.

Tana and Dario slept on an air mattress next to the dining table. I made a bed for myself at one end of the curving couch, Jan at the other.

Ethan had told us he got up at around six-thirty. Alas, he was as good as his word. *Chop, chop, chop* from the kitchen was the alarm clock. Although I tried to go on sleeping, *chop, chop, chop* continued, along with thoughts about how much I hated open plan homes. Rising at last, I got a smile and wave from Tana from where she lay on the air mattress. Staying at Ethan's was like camping with a scout troop, a mixed gender one and with the camping done indoors.

The chopping was at least in the good cause of a fruit salad, which accompanied waffles. At breakfast, Ethan sat at the head of the table. He told a string of stories, typically prefaced by, "Let me tell you a story" and ending with something like, "And how do you suppose they paid him his salary?" – how did the online gambling company based in the Isle of Wight pay the salary of the customer relations employee who lived in Berlin?

The other guests took off, Jan on Ethan's bike, which he himself hadn't used in twenty years, but kept for surfers. Seldom one to get a quick start in the morning, I hung around the loft for a while. Sitting at his computer, Ethan told me to come see the surfers who had sent him requests. He received an average of six or seven a day. He told a young woman from Asbury Park who wanted to visit New York with a girlfriend that she obviously hadn't read the instructions in his profile. "You don't give an occupation, you don't describe your education, you don't give a profile for your friend. Good luck finding a couch in New York. You'll need it." Instead of writing his messages, Ethan dictated them.

As if six or seven requests a day weren't enough, Ethan also trawled the list of Couchsurfers looking for hosts in New York. This was an alternative to writing to hosts yourself, to let them write to you. Ethan sent invitations to a couple of attractive young men. One was clearly gay, in the Couchsurfing groups for Massage, Queers, Wankers. "He's right up your alley, Ethan," I teased. However, Ethan also accepted a request from a sixty-six-year-old woman from New Zealand. "I agree to host you for three nights COMMA possibly longer COMMA if we are compatible PERIOD." Ethan had a big loft, he could accommodate other surfers along with his boy toys. "Have you had sex with any of your guests?" I asked. "A few times," he smiled.

The Slovenians made a delicious dinner for us as their thank you present to Ethan. This included dishes from their country, such as stuffed peppers and vinegary potatoes. I contributed a bottle of wine. Seated around the dining table, the group took on the feeling of a family, with Ethan as the crusty but more or less lovable grandfather. He asked us all what we'd done that day. "Did you go to Tiffany's?" he asked the Slovenians. "Did you see the Sony exhibit in the Trump Tower?" These were things he'd told them to do at breakfast, with Tana making notes.

"Let me tell you a funny story about this Polish guy," Ethan said. While yet another tale unspooled, I thought of my father at Ethan's age, seeing ever fewer of his old friends, going to a dwindling number of places. Later in the conversation, I said, "Couchsurfing could be such a great thing for older people. Think of all the stimulation they could get from meeting new people that way." Ethan didn't comment, maybe unwilling to rank himself with these older people who needed stimulation.

The Friday morning alarm clock was Ethan unloading the dishwasher. After the others had left, he asked me, "What do you think of the group?"

"It seems to be coming together," I said.

"They always do."

"You started the process by choosing the right people."

Ethan thanked me for putting the dishes in the dishwasher and cleaning the waffle iron. We seemed to have established a rapport, though I assumed he was ready to scold me again if occasion demanded.

The next day, I packed, ready to head for Boston. Seeing me to the door, Ethan told me to let him know if I returned to New York; he'd be glad to host me again. As a parting gesture, he gave my butt a squeeze.

A couple of months later, I met a young gay Indian surfer who wanted to visit New York. I suggested he send a request to Ethan. "I'm sure he'd host you at the drop of a hat." Looking for Ethan's profile, I found it had been deleted. Luckily I'd also gotten his email address. "It looks like you've deleted your profile," I wrote to him. "I hope this isn't because you had a bad experience with a guest."

Ethan shot back, "Couchsurfing deleted my profile PERIOD I wrote to them five times COMMA but they will not give me a reason PERIOD I am furious PERIOD."

Maybe Ethan had squeezed one butt too many.

ERIN AND CODY

At Ethan's loft in New York, I was a ten minute walk from Times Square. In Boston, I returned to the burbs. The Couchsurfing site advised how many hosts a surfer should write to in each location, calculating this by some sort of statistical magic: seven, nine, twelve. Making my arrangements several weeks in advance, I'd started by sending only one request for the Boston area, to a couple who sounded especially compatible, Erin and Cody. Luckily for me, they accepted. I arrived at their house as they were finishing dinner.

"Are you hungry?" Erin asked. She followed this with a question it was easier for me to answer politely: "Would you like something to eat?" I accepted a small plate of stir-fried vegetables and a couple of hard-boiled eggs, which came from their own chickens.

Erin and Cody were in their late forties. Cody was lean, fair-haired. Erin had dark hair cut sensibly short. On a chain around her neck, she wore red reading glasses that came apart at the bridge. Snapping these apart and together a hand-occupier for her, like smoking.

The house was off a quiet street on an even quieter cul-de-sac. I asked Erin and Cody if they knew their neighbors. "Yes," Erin said, "most of them. When we first moved here, our kids made friends with other kids living nearby." All wasn't totally *Leave It to Beaver*, however. Several women in the neighborhood had left their husbands. One crazy neighbor, entangled in some disagreement about the gardening allotments in a nearby park, dug up "her" dirt from the plot assigned to her and took it home.

The most sensational story was about a gay ex-cop who bought the house next door and moved in with a partner who was twenty years younger. The ex-cop was a hunter; he acquired an attack dog to protect the house. The partner a quieter type, under the other man's thumb. Erin came home one day to find police cars parked in front of the neighbors' house. She assumed at first that someone had broken in, then learned the younger partner had killed himself using one of the ex-cop's guns. "I went with Derrick to a funeral parlor to make the arrangements," Erin told me. "He'd been married when he was younger, and he told me his partner's death was God's judgment on him for indulging his homosexual tendencies."

After dinner, Cody went upstairs to practice his violin in preparation for playing at a contra dance that evening. Erin showed me around the house. The downstairs had a low beamed ceiling and a long lime-green couch. The space was decorated with African masks, old-fashioned farm tools, other interesting odds and ends. Erin said the room where I was sleeping used to be the bedroom of one of her children, Lee. On a light-switch in this room, I'd already noticed some writing in felt pen: "Lee's Room, Awesome." Lee had moved from room to room in the sprawling house. Erin showed me a room upstairs with a doll's house. Lee had used this at one time, too. As we moved away from this room, Erin mentioned that Lee was female to male transgendered. The Curious Cat was poised to pounce on Erin with questions about Lee. However, I had the impression she didn't want to discuss family matters with a near-stranger and held my tongue.

We called on Cody in his small practice room. Looking at his violin, I said, "I used to play the violin when I was a kid, though I gave it up in my twenties. I found it so much more difficult than the piano. For one thing, getting the pitch just right."

"Contra dancers mainly want a beat," Cody said. "No one is going to say, You played sharp in that passage tonight."

Lately Cody had been trying to learn classical violin as well, taking lessons from an old Romanian woman. He was progressing slowly through a few pieces. One of these was the "Meditation" from *Thais*. I offered to accompany Cody on the upright downstairs. We meditated together while Erin sat knitting nearby. I liked that we were all quickly comfortable with each other, finding ways to relate. Cody asked if we could play the piece a second time, then a third. After the third go-around, he told me that his mother, who was a pianist, refused to play things over and over with him. I said, "I have my own reasons for not wanting to play something too often. I don't know why, but my playing gets progressively worse, not better." I agreed to run through the piece just once more.

Cody invited me to the contra dance. I said I was tired and wasn't sure I wanted a late night. Erin offered to let me use her car to drive there separately. "That way, you can return before Cody if you don't want to stay the whole time."

"What a good hostess you are!" I exclaimed. "You're even offering me a car." If Erin had known I hadn't driven in nine years, she might have thought twice about this.

After Cody left, Erin showed me a binder she'd created for guests, filled with maps, articles, and the like. Next to it she kept a basket of things for their use, including some energy bars. She pointed out a tray in the refrigerator with some food for guests. Couchsurfing heaven!

We moved over to the lime-green couch, and Erin talked about her work as a life coach. "My focus is on helping people make their dreams come true. I've found that a necessary starting point is a fully formed idea, one that comes to people in a sort of vision. What doesn't usually amount to anything is some vague goal like 'I want to become rich.' One man I worked with wanted to create a program to help people in the Cameroons learn how to read. The man thought the first thing he needed to do was find some way to make a lot of money to finance the project. I helped him see that he should just start the program now, with whatever funding he had." Erin said, "If a client doesn't make progress in thirty days, I reimburse his fees."

Erin questioned me about Spain, which I'd been so smitten with after my first trip there. I kept praising it to her and hearing myself praise it. I told her about a belligerent man who had hassled me on the D.C. subway. "That would never happen in Spain." In the end, I said, "I think I want to live there." My stay in Boston involved not only Couchsurfing, but some "coach-surfing" as well.

The following morning while I had breakfast with Erin after Cody left for work, the whole Lee story came out. Erin showed me photographs of their two kids in Hawaii when they were young, Lee and Jamie. Lee a tomboy, always wanting her hair cut short. "As an adolescent, Lee said she wanted to become either a prostitute or a police officer. I told her she could become a cop who went undercover as a prostitute and fulfill both fantasies." Before entering eighth grade, Lee made a decision to switch genders. "At a school assembly, she announced that from then on, she was a he. Almost everyone accepted this, students and teachers. An exception was one of the school's crosswalk ladies. That might not have mattered so much if Lee hadn't been dating her daughter!"

Later, Lee had a mastectomy and took hormones. "If you met him now," Erin said, "you'd think he was a guy." She showed me a more recent photograph of Lee with the beginnings of a beard. "I worried about him finding partners. I shouldn't have. He's always involved with someone." Erin remarked that she and Cody had given both their kids unisex names. "We joke that we wanted to make things easier if one of them decided to have a change."

I mused on the situation. "So Lee had to switch from an Electra Complex to an Oedipus Complex."

"No," Erin said, "he always wanted to kill his father and sleep with his mother. Always hated Cody. Sometimes he'd sleep in the hall outside our room to kind of keep an eye on his rival."

Lee was adopted. In the midst of the adoption procedure, Erin became pregnant. Since she'd had many miscarriages before, she wasn't sure she would actually have this child. In the event, Jamie did arrive safely. Erin and Cody found themselves with not one, but two children, and their family life seemed all set.

As so often with real-life stories, however, there was more to it than that, even more than an adopted daughter who became a son. "Lee turned out to be a difficult child. As a teenager, he stole from Cody and me. Later, he stole jewelry from his landlady. The last straw came when he was twenty and forged my name on some checks. I said to the bank manager,

'Let's pretend for a minute it wasn't my own kid who did this. What would you advise me to do in that case?' He said, 'I'd tell you to call the police.' So that's what I did. With a criminal record, Lee found it harder to get a job. If he'd gotten through two years on probation, the authorities would have wiped his record clean. But a few months short of the two years, he was caught stealing again."

Although Lee had little contact with his birth family, Erin said he shared traits with them to an uncanny degree, as in his liking for certain foods. Another tendency was for criminal activity. Erin had talked with other adopting parents and heard similar stories about nature apparently triumphing over nurture. "Are there any ways Lee resembles you and Cody?" I asked. "Some," Erin said. "He knows how to be polite when he wants to, for one thing."

Lee wasn't in touch with Erin and Cody at present, though Erin said she was willing to talk to him if he called. Erin struck me as having found her way to a level-headed attitude toward Lee. "I learned a lot from him," she said. "He opened my eyes about gender, for one thing. I realized I'd always been a kind of masculine woman, Cody a kind of feminine man. In a controversy, I'm the one who dives in, while he hangs back."

The next morning, Erin gave me a lift to the train station. We passed the house where the man had shot himself, then the park with its rows of allotments, though I couldn't spot the one where the crazy neighbor had made off with the dirt.

Back to "Single Life is a Cabaret." I made the mistake of accepting as my singer for the event a young woman who worked at Mecca, Tori. So convenient – the manager introduced her to me at the end of the porn-themed party. At least I chose a good accompanist, Bill, whom I knew through a classical musicians group I organized. I'd become an organizer in middle age.

By the fourth rehearsal, Tori still didn't grasp that she needed to pronounce the lyrics instead of just emitting a blur of sound, usually flat. When I exclaimed, "Think of Eliza Doolittle!" she gave me a blank look. It was deflating to realize that, not only did I lack serious cultural points of reference with someone Tori's age, we didn't even share pop cultural ones. I should add in her defense that this was an art-for-art's-sake performance since, despite my nudging the manager, Mecca never agreed to pay her.

In our run-through at Mecca on the day of the party, Tori was still getting her lines mixed up. Walking around the block while I rehearsed my introduction to her, I swore I'd never host another of these parties. Swearing this had become a pre-party tradition with me. When it came time for Tori's performance, my hope that an audience would galvanize her wasn't fulfilled. She still sang flat. Only I, who had written them, could make out the lyrics to "Single Baby."

I'm just a Single Baby,
Working on the internet,
Trying to see how I can get
To be with some guy.

Running into one of the guests a few days later, he told me the singer at my party had been the worst he'd ever heard in a public setting. "Don't even bother to provide entertainment next time if that's the best you can do." On this occasion, I did fulfill my vow of never hosting another bachelor party, in part because ill-starred Mecca went out of business a couple of months later. "Single Life is a Cabaret," including its song by Stephen Sondheim with new lyrics by Gary Pedler, became just a fast fading memory in San Francisco social history.

Epilogue – Montreal

I won't beat the musical theme of this book to death by dredging one up to go with my surfing experiences in Montreal. *Rose-Marie* in any case the only possibility that comes to mind, with French Canadian Jeanette MacDonald and Mountie Nelson Eddie warbling "Indian Love Call." In the fair Francophone city, I surfed with a mother and her teenage son, a French math teacher, and a bohemian couple living in Plateau. Since I've already said a lot about my experiences as a guest, I'll turn to an aspect of Couchsurfing I haven't dealt with much yet, the local groups.

Flash forward a couple of weeks from Boston, and we find me ensconced in a new home. Two basketball players at McGill University have sublet their rooms in an apartment to me and another man for the summer. They just inherited the apartment from a couple of other guys on the team. Contrary to what they told me and the other sub-letter before they returned home to their families, I find the former tenants have disconnected the internet service. Today, a Bell technician has the WiFi working just in time for me to find a Couchsurfing group that meets this evening at six, "Québec Culture and French Language."

The notice about the meeting is rather lengthy and given first in French, then English. In a hurry, I read it quickly, gleaning mainly the essentials like time and place. This results in an evening with a succession of small surprises. The first surprise is that, instead of the bar or cafe I expect, the meeting place, Maison Viger, looks like a sober old school building. I join some people standing on the long flight of stone steps, waiting for the group leader to arrive.

One of the less happy memories of my twenties is attending social gatherings like this and hardly saying a word the whole time, too shy, too afraid. Nowadays I feel scarcely a trace of my old fear. A curly haired man on a lower step looks up at me in a clear invitation to speak. Easy. I ask him some conventional questions, like where he's from.

"Spain," he says. "Bilbao, to be precise."

"How long have you been in Montreal?"

"A few weeks."

"I've been here two." Easy. I use my rusty French and if necessary, fall back on English.

I continue chatting with Carlos, the Spaniard. Early thirties, black-framed glasses, an old-fashioned wool cap. Something likable about him. A journalist, he says he's come to Montreal to study both French and English, and to experience another culture. "The economic situation in Spain is bad," he says, "but it's better here."

More people show up. Two Iranians who've immigrated to Canada, two Argentinians passing through, a slender American woman of about my age with short black hair threaded with gray. Maxime the organizer arrives. He's a Frenchman, though he tells us that at thirty-eight, he's spent more of his life in Canada than France.

The notice about the meeting read, in slightly off English, "The event goes usually in three parts: a welcoming happy-hour time from six at the bar counter if open in order to socialize and properly introduce everyone. Followed by different work-shop tables and one-on-one individual tutoring depending on your language level and needs, one hour or so. Last, it ends with an outing to a show or an exhibition, something to let you enjoy French and Québec culture." I learn there is a bar somewhere inside the building, but we don't make it there. As for the "workshop tables," though I attend this group for the rest of the summer, these never materialize.

Instead, from Maison Viger, Maxime leads us to the Maison Symphonique, the city's symphony hall, where we catch the end of a concert by a brass quintet in the foyer. After another walk, we reach an old stone building. Maxime says something about "the opera house," yet this doesn't look like an opera house to me. He gives us a choice between attending a song recital here or continuing on to Parc La Fontaine for a *pique-nique littéraire*. The latter apparently involves a book discussion, though through the slight haze of French, I'm unsure about this. Not wanting to walk any farther, while most of the others head for the park with Maxime, I opt for the recital, as do Carlos and Jessica, the American woman.

Inside, a young woman tells us the recital started ten minutes ago, but that we can slip in and find seats when there's a pause. The three of us wait together on a bench. Jessica says she's hungry. This is her first time with the group, as it is Carlos's and mine, and she didn't realize we wouldn't have a chance to eat anything during the evening. I fish out of my shoulder bag one of the protein bars the basketball players left behind. Jessica accepts this offer gratefully. "Are you hungry?" I ask Carlos. "No, I'm thirsty," he says. "I saw a drinking fountain over there," I tell him. I lead him to it. I'm pleased to have satisfied the hunger of Jessica and the thirst of Carlos.

Carlos tells me he's writing a book. Jessica pipes up that she's writing one, too. I ask Jessica what kind of work she does. "That's something I'm trying to figure out," she smiles, "what kind I want to do, which path to pursue out of several." Something likable about her as well.

The young woman ushers us inside the theater. Jessica leads the way past the tiered seats on the ground floor and up a flight of stairs to a gallery running around three sides of the narrow hall. We sit almost in the center of the back. Clearly we aren't in an opera house. Looking at the program, I read that this was originally the chapel of a monastery. The young singers giving the recital come from Montreal Opera's Atelier Lyrique. It's an all Poulenc program.

Let's imagine the scene through a camera slowly panning down. From the ceiling with its plaster rosettes, our frame of vision descends a chain, then the chandelier it supports, tier by tier. Four tiers altogether, like four fountains spraying water. Still farther down, six gold-tinted lights amid more sprays. The chandelier must be crystal, any other material seems unlikely, yet from where we sit, perhaps because of clever lighting, it looks like it's made of gold dotted with globs of silver. Now we reach the raised lid of the grand piano, reflecting the pale interior. The reflective piano is reflected in its turn by the polished wooden floor, its sleek black body and three gleaming gold feet.

An Asian woman is seated at the piano. Her evening dress extends down to her feet, but only rises as far as the top of her breasts. By contrast, the soprano's green silk skirt shows her legs to several inches above the knees while concealing her upper body. After a group of songs, the two women are replaced by two men, a tenor and another pianist. This pattern continues with an alto, then a bass, as if the recital is designed so that only the Female will hold the stage or the Male, with no dilution.

It's difficult to turn from the rapidly changing kaleidoscopes of movies and television to something like this recital, where very little changes from one moment to the next. Yet this lack of change helps fix every single thing in my mind. The swan-neck movement with which one of the female pianists lifts her hands from the keys. The way the tenor places a hand on the piano and turns his head away to mark the change of mood from one song to another.

Song succeeds song, some sad, some witty. Several I've heard before, others not. I catch a few of the words, miss many. I can hear Carlos breathing to my left. To my right, I see out of the corner of my eye Jessica writing in a notebook. Will the recital appear in the book she's writing, as I anticipate it will appear in this one of mine, viewed from a different angle and serving a different narrative purpose? Later, I see she's sketching the chandelier, so at least it's clear we've both been struck by it. I sense in Jessica a kindred spirit, noticing how carefully she studies the program, other small things. She seems like a person who wants to improve herself and make something special out of her life.

As the recital continues, I wish the singers would combine their voices rather than always singing solos. Finally, in the last number, they oblige, standing in a row for a quartet version of "*Les Chemins de l'amour*," "The Paths of Love." Poulenc's music is never very knotty. "*Les Chemins*" comes especially close to a popular style, sounding like a song from an operetta – or even a musical. A song you could sing in the shower or, with its steady waltz rhythm, dance to around a ballroom.

The word *chemins* appears again and again in the song, referring to paths of love, distress, memory. This makes me think of the many *chemins* I've traveled during the last four months, the sidewalks, streets, railroad tracks, airplane flight-paths. How many intercoms have I buzzed, doorbells rung, knockers rapped, and how many doors have opened for me. If I ever imagined this trip would be a matter of monuments and museums, meals and views, I was wrong. Looking back, these are small features on the paths, and it's the human encounters that loom large. If I ever thought Couchsurfing was just cheap and convenient, I was wrong about this as well. I turn over in my mind all the gifts my hosts have given me, memories, experiences, and yes, some challenges. I hope I've given them something in return; again, on occasion, perhaps a bit of a challenge. "Gary was a little," fill in the blank, "but on the whole, I did enjoy his visit." Dependent on the kindness of strangers to a high degree, I've been passed from the hand of one to another, down a long line and always safely, as it turned out. How are all my hosts at this moment? What are they doing, thinking? I can't collect them in the same room, though at least I can begin to imagine bringing them together in these pages.

After the recital, Jessica, Carlos, and I linger on the sidewalk. The evening has been a strange journey, around the city, which I still don't know well, in and out of buildings. The weather has made its own voyage, starting so hot I arrived in shorts, later cooling, clouding up, even tossing down some rain. I want to see both Jessica and Carlos again. This turns out to be simple. Parting, we ask each other if we plan to come to the group next week. We all say yes.

The three writers do return the following week. I become friends with Jessica and Carlos, who keep me company on the path leading across my summer in Montreal. We attend the Wednesday group and also see each other outside it. We wonder when the group will ever run according to the notice posted on the website, including all three of the parts described. It never does.

END

Photo by Mary Muszynski

About the Author

Gary has written two adult novels, a YA novel, two story collections, and, a little to his surprise, a play. A resident of San Francisco for longer than he cares to admit, Gary qualifies as a true Bay Area denizen. Yet after a recent escape from his white-collar wage slave job, he's spent much of his time rambling around the world and, of course, writing about everything he sees. Find out more about Gary at www.garypedler.com.

48190034R00139

Printed in Poland
by Amazon Fulfillment
Poland Sp. z o.o., Wrocław